I0023077

W. S. Hoyte

A Book of Litanies Metrical and Prose

W. S. Hoyte

A Book of Litanies Metrical and Prose

ISBN/EAN: 9783337372484

Printed in Europe, USA, Canada, Australia, Japan

Cover: Foto ©Thomas Meinert / pixelio.de

More available books at **www.hansebooks.com**

A

BOOK OF LITANIES

Metrical and Prose

WITH

AN EVENING SERVICE

AND

ACCOMPANYING MUSIC

ARRANGED UNDER THE MUSICAL EDITORSHIP

OF

W. S. HOYTE

ORGANIST AND DIRECTOR OF THE CHOIR AT ALL SAINTS', MARGARET STREET, LONDON

RIVINGTONS

London, Oxford, and Cambridge

1875

PREFACE

THE EDITOR of this "BOOK OF LITANIES" desires to avail himself of the opportunity afforded him, in issuing the Words with the Music, to thank those persons who have contributed Litanies, those who have so kindly helped him with much valuable advice and criticism in the preparation of the Words, and those who have generously placed Litanies already published at his disposal. He desires especially to thank the Writer of the Metrical Litanies for Advent, Penitence (p. 10), Rogation Days, Whitsuntide (p. 38), Saints' Days, and of the two on the Passion, for his permission to insert them. His best acknowledgments are also due to the Rev. J. E. FIELD for allowing him to use his translation of a Metrical Litany from the Mozarabic Missal as a "Litany in any Calamity."

The accompanying Music will, it is hoped, be found in every way a suitable vehicle for the Words; and the EDITOR, in addition to acknowledging in the Index the authorship of the various Tunes, desires here to thank all who have so materially contributed by their work, as well as by the interest that they have taken in it, to the value of the Book. To Mr. W. S. HOYTE, the Musical Editor, he would offer his best thanks for the skill and judgment with which he has prepared the Music for the press, for his Tunes, as well as for his harmonies to the foreign Airs; to Mr. WILLIAM JAMES, Organist of

St. Andrew's Kenn, Exeter, for his Tunes and for the great care and labour that he has bestowed upon the work that he has done for the Book; and to the Rev. J. B. DYKES, M.A., Mus. Doc., Vicar of St. Oswald's, Durham; the Rev. H. H. WOODWARD, M.A., Mus. Bac.; Dr. STAINER, M.A., the Organist of St. Paul's Cathedral; and Mr. BERTHOLD TOURS, for the Tunes which they have contributed, as well as for the help and advice which they have given from time to time. He desires also, in addition to the above-named, to thank the Right Rev. Bishop JENNER; Professor W. H. MONK, of King's College, London; Dr. GAUNTLETT; Mr. E. H. THORNE; Mr. J. WARWICK JORDAN; Mr. R. N. MANT; Mr. GERARD F. COBB; and Mr. J. KNIGHT BAKER, for their kindness in writing Tunes expressly for the Book; and for the use of Tunes that have been already published, the Rev. W. PLOWS; Mr. J. WHITAKER; the Authoress of "Twelve Litanies by E. R. B." (Novello); and Messrs. BURNS & OATES (for Tunes from the "Choir Manual").

This Book of Litanies is now issued, in the hope that it may be one more help to the use of that form of devotion which has, from the earliest ages of the Church, been found at special times and seasons to meet a want of the soul in prayer, which no other form can adequately supply.

Easter, 1875.

CONTENTS

METRICAL LITANIES

PAGE

Litany for Advent—No. I 1
Litany for Advent—No. II 6
Litany of Penitence—No. I 10
Litany of Penitence—No. II 14
Litany of the Passion—No. I 18
Litany of the Passion—No. II 22
Litany of the Resurrection 26
Litany for Rogation Days 30
Litany of the Ascension 34
Litany of the Holy Ghost—No. I 38
Litany of the Holy Ghost—No. II 42
Litany of the Holy Ghost—No. III 46
Litany of our Lord Jesus Christ 50
Litany for Saints' Days 54
Litany of the Holy Angels 58
Litany for the Church 62
Litany of the Blessed Sacrament ... 66
Litany of the Holy Childhood 70
Litany in any Calamity 74
Litany for a Happy Death 78

PROSE LITANIES

Litany for Advent 82
Litany of Penitence... 86
Litany of the Passion 90
Litany of the Resurrection ... 94
Litany of the Ascension 98
Litany of the Holy Ghost ... 102
Litany of the Holy Name of Jesus 106
Litany for Saints' Days ... 110
Litany of the Holy Angels ... 114
Litany for the Church 118
Litany of the Blessed Sacrament 122
Litany of the Holy Child Jesus... 126
Litany for a Happy Death ... 128
AN EVENING SERVICE ... 132

GENERAL INDEX

			PAGE
ADVENT, Litany for, No. I	(Metrical) ...	...	1
„ „ No. II ...	(Metrical) ...	...	6
„ „	(Prose) ...	...	82
ASCENSION, Litany of the	(Metrical) ...	...	34
„ „ „	(Prose) ...	...	98
BLESSED SACRAMENT, Litany of the	(Metrical) ...	...	66
„ „ „ ...	(Prose) ...	...	122
CALAMITY, Litany in any	(Metrical) ...	...	74
CHURCH, Litany for the	(Metrical) ...	...	62
„ „	(Prose) ...	...	118
HAPPY DEATH, Litany for a ...	(Metrical) ...	...	78
„ „	(Prose) ...	...	128
HOLY ANGELS, Litany of the ...	(Metrical) ...	...	58
„ „	(Prose) ...	...	114
HOLY CHILDHOOD, Litany of the ...	(Metrical) ...	...	70
HOLY CHILD JESUS, Litany of the ...	(Prose) ...	...	126
HOLY GHOST, Litany of the, No. I	(Metrical) ..	...	38
„ „ No. II	(Metrical) ...	...	42
„ „ No. III	(Metrical) ...	...	46
„ „	(Prose) ...	...	102
HOLY NAME OF JESUS, Litany of the	(Prose) ...	...	106
JESUS CHRIST, Litany of OUR LORD	(Metrical) ...	...	50
PASSION, Litany of the, No. I ...	(Metrical) ...	...	18
„ „ No. II ...	(Metrical) ...	...	22
„ „ ...	(Prose) ...	...	90
PENITENCE, Litany of, No. I ...	(Metrical) ...	...	10
„ „ No. II ...	(Metrical) ...	...	14
„ „ ...	(Prose) ...	...	86
RESURRECTION, Litany of the ...	(Metrical) ...	...	26
„ „ ...	(Prose) ...	...	94
ROGATION DAYS, Litany for... ...	(Metrical) ...	...	30
SAINTS' DAYS, Litany for	(Metrical) ...	...	54
„ „	(Prose) ...	...	110
AN EVENING SERVICE		...	132

INDEX OF TUNES

This Collection of Litanies is copyright, and for permission to reprint any of the Litanies or Tunes, or Harmonies to the Tunes, or to the Music of the Evening Service, application should be made to the Editor, care of Messrs. Rivington.

METRICAL LITANIES

LITANY	COMPOSER OF TUNE	PAGE
Advent, For—No. I ...	H. J. GAUNTLETT, Mus. Doc. ...	1
Advent, For—No. II	Rev. J. B. DYKES, M.A., Mus. Doc.	6
Ascension, Of the		
First Tune	Twelve Litanies by E. R. B ...	34
Second Tune ...	WILLIAM JAMES	36
Blessed Sacrament, Of the ...	Rev. J. B. DYKES, M.A., Mus. Doc.	66
Calamity, In any		
First Tune	Rev. J. B. DYKES, M.A., Mus. Doc.	74
Second Tune ...	WILLIAM JAMES	76
Church, For the		
First Tune	CHOIR MANUAL, harmonized by W. S. HOYTE ...	62
Second Tune ...	ANONYMOUS	63
Third Tune	CHOIR MANUAL, harmonized by W. S. HOYTE ...	64
Happy Death, For a		
First Tune ...	J. KNIGHT BAKER	78
Second Tune ...	Foreign, harmonized by W. S. HOYTE ...	79
Third Tune ...	CHOIR MANUAL, harmonized by W. S. HOYTE ...	80
Holy Angels, Of the		
First Tune ...	BERTHOLD TOURS ...	58
Second Tune ...	W. S. HOYTE	60
Holy Childhood, Of the		
First Tune ...	Foreign, harmonized by W. S. HOYTE	70
Second Tune	R. N. MANT ...	72
Holy Ghost, Of the—No. I		
First Tune	W. S. HOYTE	38
Second Tune	BERTHOLD TOURS ...	40
Holy Ghost, Of the—No. II		
First Tune	Professor W. H. MONK	42
Second Tune	Rev. H. H. WOODWARD, M.A., Mus. Bac.	44
Holy Ghost, Of the—No. III		
First Tune	MOZART, arranged by W. S. HOYTE	46
Second Tune ...	J. WARWICK JORDAN, Mus. Bac. ...	48

LITANY	COMPOSER OF TUNE	PAGE
Jesus Christ, Of our Lord		
First Tune ...	Foreign, harmonized by W. S. Hoyte ...	50
Second Tune ...	Choir Manual, harmonized by W. S. Hoyte ...	51
Third Tune ...	Foreign, harmonized by W. S. Hoyte ...	52
Passion, Of the—No. I		
First Tune ...	Gerard F. Cobb, M.A., Fellow of Trin. Coll., Cambridge	18
Second Tune ...	J. Stainer, M.A., Mus. Doc.	20
Passion, Of the—No. II		
First Tune ...	Foreign, harmonized by W. S. Hoyte	22
Second Tune ...	E. H. Thorne	24
Penitence, Of—No. I		
First Tune ...	Rev. J. B. Dykes, M.A., Mus. Doc.	10
Second Tune ...	W. S. Hoyte	12
Penitence, Of—No. II		
First Tune ...	Rev. W. Plows, M.A.	14
Second Tune ...	Foreign, harmonized by W. S. Hoyte ...	16
Resurrection, Of the		
First Tune ...	Choir Manual, harmonized by W. S. Hoyte ...	26
Second Tune ...	Rev. H. H. Woodward M.A., Mus. Bac. ...	27
Third Tune ...	Choir Manual, harmonized by W. S. Hoyte ...	28
Rogation Days, For		
First Tune ...	Foreign, harmonized by W. S. Hoyte	30
Second Tune ...	J. Whitaker	32
Saints' Days, For		
First Tune	W. S. Hoyte	54
Second Tune ...	Choir Manual, harmonized by W. S. Hoyte ...	55
Third Tune ...	William James	56

PROSE LITANIES

Advent, For ...	Foreign, harmonized by W. S. Hoyte ...	82
Ascension, Of the ...	Foreign, harmonized by W. S. Hoyte ...	98
Blessed Sacrament, Of the	Rev. H. H. Woodward, M.A., Mus. Bac.	122
Church, For the ...	W. S. Hoyte	118
Happy Death, For a	Foreign, harmonized by W. S. Hoyte	128
Holy Angels, Of the	Foreign, harmonized by W. S. Hoyte ...	114
Holy Child Jesus, Of the ...	Foreign, harmonized by W. S. Hoyte ...	126
Holy Ghost, Of the...	William James	102
Holy Name, Of the	Right Rev. Bishop Jenner	106
Passion, Of the	W. S. Hoyte	90
Penitence, Of	Foreign, harmonized by W. S. Hoyte ...	86
Resurrection, Of the	Foreign, harmonized by W. S. Hoyte ...	94
Saints' Days, For	Foreign, harmonized by W. S. Hoyte ...	110
AN EVENING SERVICE	Harmonized and arranged by W. S. Hoyte	132

LITANIES ARRANGED FOR USE THROUGHOUT THE CHURCH'S YEAR

			PAGE
Advent	For Advent	(Metrical)	1-6
	For Advent	(Prose)	82
	For a Happy Death	(Metrical)	78
	For a Happy Death	(Prose)	128
Christmas	Of the Holy Childhood	(Metrical)	70
	Of our Lord—Parts I, III	(Metrical)	50
Circumcision	Of the Holy Name	(Prose)	106
	Of the Holy Child Jesus	(Prose)	126
Epiphany	Of our Lord—Parts I, III	(Metrical)	50
Lent	Of Penitence—No. I	(Metrical)	10
	„ No. II	(Metrical)	14
	Of Penitence	(Prose)	86
	Of the Passion—No. I	(Metrical)	18
	„ No. II	(Metrical)	22
	Of the Passion	(Prose)	90
	Of our Lord—Parts I, IV	(Metrical)	50
Easter	For Easter	(Metrical)	26
	For Easter	(Prose)	94
Rogation Days	For Rogation Days	(Metrical)	30
Ascension Tide	Of the Ascension	(Metrical)	34
	Of the Ascension	(Prose)	98
Whitsuntide	Of the Holy Ghost—No. I	(Metrical)	38
	„ „ No. II	(Metrical)	42
	„ „ No. III	(Metrical)	46
	Of the Holy Ghost	(Prose)	102
Ember Days	Of the Holy Ghost—No. I	(Metrical)	38
	„ „ No. II	(Metrical)	42
	Of the Holy Ghost	(Prose)	102
	For the Church	(Metrical)	62
	For the Church	(Prose)	118
Trinity	Of our Lord Jesus Christ	(Metrical)	50
	For Rogation Days	(Metrical)	30
Saints' Days	For Saints' Days	(Metrical)	54
	For Saints' Days	(Prose)	110
Michaelmas	Of the Holy Angels	(Metrical)	58
	Of the Holy Angels	(Prose)	114

LITANIES ARRANGED FOR DIFFERENT OCCASIONS

Foreign Missions	For the Church	(Metrical)	62
	For the Church	(Prose)	118
	Of the Holy Ghost—No. I	(Metrical)	38
	„ „ No. II	(Metrical)	42
Mourners	For a Happy Death—Parts I, IV	(Metrical)	78
War, Famine, Pestilence	In any Calamity	(Metrical)	74

SUGGESTIONS WITH REGARD TO THE USE OF THE WORDS AND MUSIC OF THE METRICAL LITANIES

1. The Verse may be sung by the Priest or Two Cantors, or Priest with One Cantor; the Choir and Congregation joining in the Response.

2. The Verses may be sung antiphonally by the Choir and Congregation, the whole Congregation with the Full Choir joining in the Responses: the first and last Verses being sung by the Full Choir and the whole Congregation.

3. The first Verse may be sung by the Priest or Two Cantors, or Priest with One Cantor; the Choir and Congregation singing the Response, as well as the next Verse, with the Response: the last Verse being sung by the Full Choir and Congregation.

4. The small notes in the last bar of some of the Tunes are intended for the First Response only of the Litany, viz., "Hear us, HOLY TRINITY."

Advent

LITANY FOR ADVENT—No. 1

Choir
Priest or Two Cantors
LORD, have mer - cy.
LORD, have mer - cy.
Priest
Choir
Priest
Choir
CHRIST, have mer-cy.
CHRIST, have mer-cy.
LORD, have mer-cy.
LORD, have mer - cy.
Priest
FA - THER E - ter - nal, GOD Most High, CHRIST to our race in flesh made nigh,
SPI - RIT, Who dost all grace sup - ply;
Choir
Hear us, O GOD, we pray.

Priest
Je - su, . . the wo-man's promised Seed, Bruis - er . . for us of the serpent's head,
Hope . . of the Patriarch's dy - ing bed;
Choir
Hear us, O God, we pray.

PRESENCE revealed in the bush of flame,
Rock whence the waters freely came,
Known by Jehovah's awful Name;
Hear us, O God, we pray.

Sceptre and Star and Diadem,
Plant of renown from Jesse's stem,
King that wast born in Bethlehem;
Hear us, O God, we pray.

Thou Whom Isaiah's awe-struck eye
Saw on Thy throne of light most high,
Saw on this earth condemned to die;
Hear us, O God, we pray.

SAVIOUR of Whom the prophets speak,
With silent lip and smitten cheek,
Man of sorrows, Redeemer meek;
Hear us, O God, we pray.

King of the world beyond the skies,
Dwelling with us in earthly guise,
With voice of love and pitying eyes;
Hear us, O God, we pray.

JESU, great and adorèd Name,
Glorified now through Thy death of shame,
JESU for evermore the Same;
Hear us, O God, we pray.

Priest
Word and Wis - dom of God Most High, Ru - ling in sweet - est har - mo - ny

All the years of e - ter - ni - ty;
Choir
Come and re-deem, O Lord.

LORD and Leader of Israel's line,
Shewn to Moses in fiery sign,
Able to save by might divine;
Come and redeem, O LORD.

Root of Jesse, before Whose sway
Kings shall be silent and obey,
Thou to Whom Gentile nations pray;
Come and redeem, O LORD.

Key of David, Who evermore
Opening wide the heavenly door
Wilt to our darkness light restore;
Come and redeem, O LORD.

Splendour of everlasting light,
Overcoming the shades of night,
Sun of righteousness, Dayspring bright;
Come and redeem, O LORD.

King of the Gentiles, and their Desire,
Mighty to save from eternal fire
All whom with life Thou dost inspire;
Come and redeem, O LORD.

O Emmanuel, SAVIOUR, King,
Who by Thy merits ransoming
Dost the new law to Thy people bring;
Come and redeem, O LORD.

III

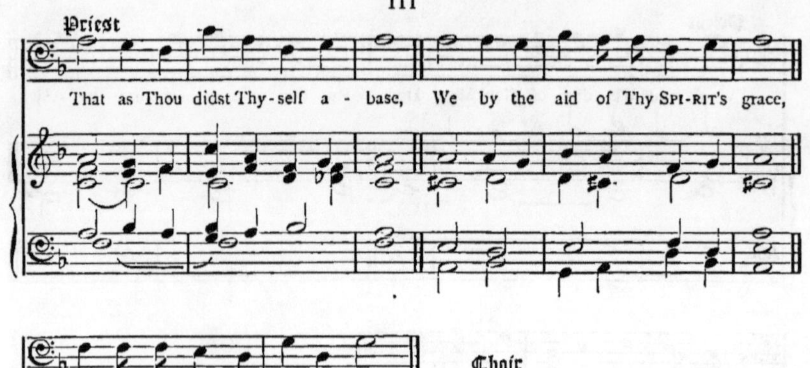
Priest
That as Thou didst Thy-self a - base, We by the aid of Thy SPI-RIT's grace,

E - ver may choose the low - est place,
Choir
Hear us, O GOD, we pray.

THAT in the strength of Thy promise sure,
We, Thy servants, faithful and pure,
May to the end of our race endure,
Hear us, O GOD, we pray.

That Thou wouldst kindle hope divine,
Granting to souls that are knit to Thine
Visions bright of Thy face benign,
Hear us, O GOD, we pray.

That in the Day of Thine Advent dread
We with the sheep may be numbered,
So to the living waters led,
Hear us, O GOD, we pray.

That Thou wouldst cleanse our dazzled sight,
Making it bear the radiance bright
Shed by Thine everlasting light,
Hear us, O GOD, we pray.

That when we stand before Thy throne
Thou wouldst accept us as Thine own,
Thine for eternity, Thine alone,
Hear us, O GOD, we pray.

Priest
LORD, have mer-cy.
Choir
LORD, have mer-cy.
Priest
CHRIST, have mer-cy.
Choir
CHRIST, have mer-cy.

Priest
LORD, have mer-cy.
Choir
LORD, have mer - cy.
Priest
Our FATHER.
Choir
A - men.
Priest
℣ The night is far spent, The day is at hand;
Choir
℟ Let us there-fore cast off the works of dark - ness, and let us put
on the ar - mour of light.
Priest
Let us pray.

Almighty God, give us grace that we may cast away the works of darkness, and put upon us the armour of light, now in the time of this mortal life, in which Thy Son Jesus Christ came to visit us in great humility; that in the last day, when He shall come again in His glorious majesty to judge both the quick and dead, we may rise to the life immortal; through Him Who liveth and reigneth with Thee and the Holy Ghost, now and ever.

Choir

A - men.

LITANY FOR ADVENT—No. II

Priest or Two Cantors
Choir
Lord, have mer - cy.
Lord, have mer - cy.
Priest
Choir
Priest
Choir
Christ, have mer-cy.
Christ, have mer-cy.
Lord, have mer-cy.
Lord, have mer - cy.
I
Verse
Fa-ther E - ter - nal, God most high, Christ to our race in flesh made nigh,
Response
Spi - rit, Who dost all grace sup - ply; . . Hear us, O God, we pray. . . .

Jesu, the woman's promised Seed,
Bruiser for us of the serpent's head,
Hope of the Patriarch's dying bed;
Hear us, O God, we pray.

Presence revealed in the bush of flame,
Rock whence the waters freely came,
Known by Jehovah's awful Name;
Hear us, O God, we pray.

Sceptre and Star and Diadem,
Plant of renown from Jesse's stem,
King that wast born in Bethlehem;
Hear us, O God, we pray.

Thou Whom Isaiah's awe-struck eye,
Saw on Thy throne of light most high,
Saw on this earth condemned to die;
Hear us, O God, we pray.

Saviour of Whom the Prophets speak,
With silent lip and smitten cheek,
Măn of sorrows, Redeemer meek;
Hear us, O God, we pray.

King of the world beyond the skies,
Dwelling with us in earthly guise,
With voice of love and pitying eyes;
Hear us, O God, we pray.

Jësu, great and adorèd Name,
Glorified now through Thy death of shame,
Jesu for evermore the Same;
Hear us, O God, we pray.

II

Verse
Word and Wis-dom of God most high, Ru-ling in sweet-est har - mo - ny

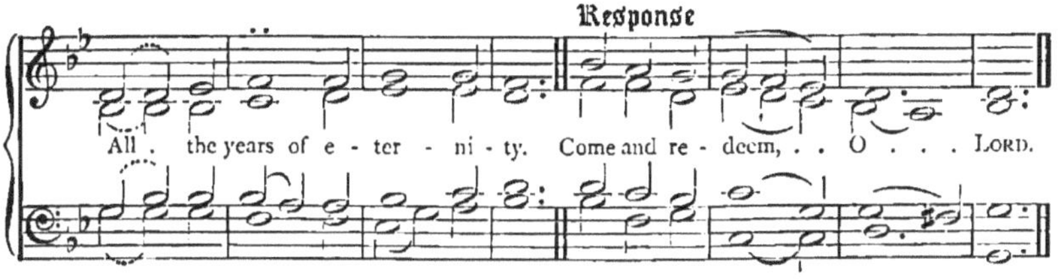
All . the years of e - ter - ni - ty.
Response
Come and re - deem, . . O . . . Lord.

LORD and Leader of Israel's line,
 Shewn to Moses in fiery sign,
Able to save by might divine;
 Come and redeem, O Lord.

Root of Jesse, before Whose sway .
Kings shall be silent and obey,
Thou to Whom Gentile nations pray;
 Come and redeem, O Lord.

Key of David, Who evermore
Opening wide the heavenly door
Wilt to our darkness light restore;
 Come and redeem, O Lord.

Splendour of everlasting light,
Overcoming the shades of night,
Sun of Righteousness, Dayspring bright;
 Come and redeem, O Lord.

King of the Gentiles, and their Desire,
Mighty to save from eternal fire
All whom with life Thou dost inspire;
 Come and redeem, O Lord.

O Emmanuel, Saviour, King,
Who by Thy merits ransoming
Dost the new law to Thy people bring;
 Come and redeem, O Lord.

III

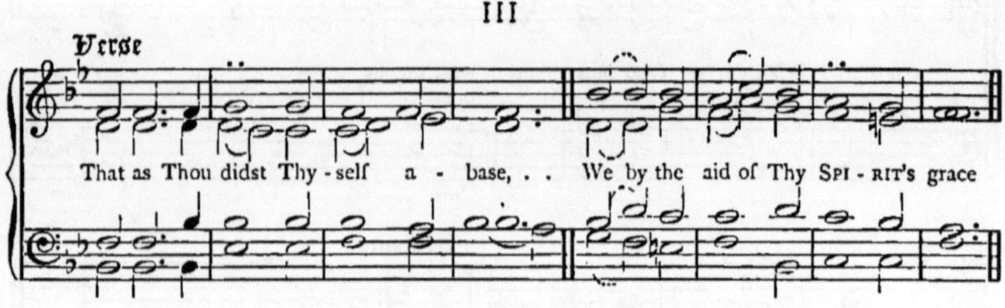
Verse
That as Thou didst Thy - self a - base, . . We by the aid of Thy Spi - rit's grace

Response
E - ver may choose the low - est place, Hear us, O God, we pray. . .

That in the strength of Thy promise sure,
We, Thy servants, faithful and pure,
May to the end of our race endure,
Hear us, O God, we pray.

That Thou wouldst kindle hope divine,
Granting to souls that are knit to Thine
Visions bright of Thy face benign,
Hear us, O God, we pray.

That in the Day of Thine Advent dread
We with the sheep may be numbered,
So to the living waters led,
Hear us, O God, we pray.

That Thou wouldst cleanse our dazzled sight,
Making it bear the radiance bright
Shed by Thine everlasting light,
Hear us, O God, we pray.

That when we stand before Thy throne
Thou wouldst accept us as Thine own,
Thine for eternity, Thine alone,
Hear us, O God, we pray.

Priest

LORD, have mer - cy.

Choir

LORD, have mer - cy.

Priest

CHRIST, have mer-cy.

Choir

CHRIST, have mer-cy.

Priest

LORD, have mer-cy.

Choir

LORD, have mer - cy.

Priest

Our FATHER.

Priest

℣ The night is far spent, the day is at hand.

Choir

℟ Let us therefore cast off the works of dark - ness, and let us put on the ar - mour of light. . .

Priest

Let us pray.

ALMIGHTY GOD, give us grace that we may cast away the works of darkness, and put upon us the armour of light, now in the time of this mortal life, in which Thy SON JESUS CHRIST came to visit us in great humility; that in the last day, when He shall come again in His glorious majesty to judge both the quick and dead, we may rise to the life immortal; through Him Who liveth and reigneth with Thee and the HOLY GHOST, now and ever.

Choir

A - men.

Lent

LITANY OF PENITENCE—No. I

Choir
Priest or Two Cantors
LORD, have mer - cy.
LORD, have mer - cy.
Choir
Priest
CHRIST, have mer - cy.
CHRIST, have mer - cy.
Choir
Priest
LORD, have mer - - - - cy.
LORD, have mer - cy.
Verse—FIRST TUNE
Response

LORD, have mercy.
CHRIST, have mercy.
LORD, have mercy.

FATHER, Whose love we have wronged by transgression,
CHRIST, Who wast nailed for our sins on the Tree,
SPIRIT, Who givest the grace of repentance;
Hear us, we pray Thee, Good LORD.

JESU, Adorable SAVIOUR of sinners,
Author of penitence, Hope of our souls,
Plentiful Fountain of grace and compassion;
Hear us, we pray Thee, Good LORD.

I

THOU Who condemning the reprobate Angels
Gavest them up to the doom of their choice,
Awful example of endless perdition;
Hear us, we pray Thee, Good LORD.

Seed of the woman, Whose promise of mercy
Shining on man in the gloom of his fall,
Holding us back from despair and damnation;
Hear us, we pray Thee, Good LORD.

Thou Who didst save from the midst of the wicked
Noah Thy servant, who witnessed for Thee,
Faithfully building the ark of salvation;
Hear us, we pray Thee, Good LORD.

Thou Who, o'erthrowing the city of Sodom,
Lot by the hands of Thine Angels didst send
Safely away to the mountain of refuge;
Hear us, we pray Thee, Good LORD.

Thou Who hast taught us the love of the Father,
Meeting with mercy the prodigal son
Weary of sin and abased in confession;
Hear us, we pray Thee, Good LORD.

Thou Who didst enter the house of Zaccheus,
Blessing his faith and accepting his love,
When with his riches he made restitution;
Hear us, we pray Thee, Good LORD.

Thou Who hast willed that not any should perish,
But to repentance that all men should come,
Saved by the Blood of Thy precious Atonement;
Hear us, we pray Thee, Good LORD.

Judge of the world, that before Thy tribunal
We may find mercy and pardon from Thee,
Judged by ourselves in our time of probation;
Hear us, we pray Thee, Good LORD.

II

THOU Who didst empty Thyself of Thy glory,
Thou Who Thy parents on earth didst obey;
That by Thy meekness our pride may be vanquished,
Hear us, we pray Thee, Good LORD.

That from the love of the world and its riches
Thou wouldst preserve us and make us Thine own,
Following Thee in Thy life of privation,
Hear us, we pray Thee, Good LORD.

That through Thy fasting and awful temptation
We may be fed by the Word of our GOD,
Sober in food and restrained in enjoyment,
Hear us, we pray Thee, Good LORD.

Lamb without spot, everlastingly holy,
Thou Who wast born of a Virgin most pure,
That Thou wouldst save us from all that defileth,
Hear us, we pray Thee, Good LORD.

CHRIST in one Body Who bindest Thy members,
Lover of all men, Whom all men must love,
That Thou wouldst keep us from envy and hatred,
Hear us, we pray Thee, Good LORD.

Thou Who wast silent when malice assailed Thee,
Meek and unmoved in the midst of Thy foes,
That we may never give way to our anger,
Hear us, we pray Thee, Good LORD.

O by Thy days of unwearying labour,
O by Thy watchings and prayers in the night,
That in Thy service we ne'er may be slothful,
Hear us, we pray Thee, Good LORD.

Sins of the past which we fail to remember,
Sins which in sorrow we meekly confess,
That by Thy love they may all be forgiven,
Hear us, we pray Thee, Good LORD.

Verse—Second Tune
Response

III

JESU, Who once by the well to the sinner
Clearly the sins of her heart didst reveal,
That Thou wouldst lead us to see our transgressions,
Hear us, we pray Thee, Good LORD.

JESU, Whose look of ineffable sorrow
Melted the heart that in vain Thou hadst warned,
That Thou wouldst give us the grace of contrition,
Hear us, we pray Thee, Good LORD.

Thou Who, dismissing the crowd and the minstrels,
Calledst the child of the Ruler to life,
That Thou wouldst raise us from death and damnation,
Hear us, we pray Thee, Good LORD.

Thou Who dost sit as the mighty Refiner
Silver and gold in the furnace to try,
That Thou wouldst purge us from earthly corruption,
Hear us, we pray Thee, Good LORD.

That we may fall at Thy feet and adore Thee,
Pouring before Thee the gifts of our love,
Knowing Thy power and trusting Thy mercy,
Hear us, we pray Thee, Good LORD.

That we may bring forth works meet for repentance,
That we give place to the devil no more,
That Thou wouldst lead us to full perseverance,
Hear us, we pray Thee, Good LORD.

That we may work out with fear our salvation,
That we may put on the armour of GOD,
That we may live to Thy righteousness only,
Hear us, we pray Thee, Good LORD.

That in this life Thou wouldst purge our transgressions,
Giving us grace to submit to Thy love,
So in the day of Thy wrath Thou mayst spare us,
Hear us, we pray Thee, Good LORD.

Priest
Lord, have mer - cy.
Choir
Lord, have mer - cy.
Priest
Christ, have mer - cy.
Choir
Christ, have mer - cy.
Priest
Lord, have mer - cy.
Choir
Lord, have mer - - - - cy.
Priest
Our Father.
Priest
℣ Create in us a clean heart, O God.
Choir
℟ And renew a right spi - rit with - in . . . . . us.
Priest
Let us pray.
Choir
A - men.

ALMIGHTY and Everlasting God, Who hatest nothing that Thou hast made, and dost forgive the sins of all them that are penitent; create and make in us new and contrite hearts, that we worthily lamenting our sins, and acknowledging our wretchedness, may obtain of Thee, the God of all mercy, perfect remission and forgiveness; through Jesus Christ our Lord.

Choir
Priest or Two Cantors
LORD, have mer - cy.
LORD, have mer - cy.
Choir
Priest
CHRIST, have mer - cy.
CHRIST, have mer - cy.
Choir
Priest
LORD, have mer - cy.
LORD, have mer - cy.
Verse—FIRST TUNE
Response

LORD, have mercy.
CHRIST, have mercy.
LORD, have mercy.

GOD the FATHER, GOD the SON,
GOD the SPIRIT, Three in One,
In the hope of pardon won;
Hear us, Holy TRINITY.

CHRIST, Whose mercy guideth still
Sinners from the paths of ill,
Teaching them to do Thy will;
Hear us, Holy JESU.

I

THOU Who, when the Angels fell,
Sparedst not, but doomed to hell
Hurledst them in woe to dwell;
Hear us, Holy JESU.

Thou Who, when through Satan's art
Adam fell, didst pierce his heart
With remorse's healing smart;
Hear us, Holy JESU.

Thou Who Pharaoh's pride didst smite,
Taking vengeance in Thy might,
On that much remembered night;
Hear us, Holy JESU.

Thou Who, in Thy loving care,
At Thy faithful Prophet's prayer,
Didst rebellious Israel spare;
Hear us, Holy JESU.

Thou Whose word to David sent,
When from Thy right ways he went,
Made the sinner penitent;
Hear us, Holy JESU.

Thou Who bowedst down Thine ear
Prostrate Nineveh to hear,
Faint with fasting, grief, and fear;
Hear us, Holy JESU.

Thou Who from Thy heavenly throne
Soughtst the earth, an Outcast lone,
That Thou mightest save Thine own;
Hear us, Holy JESU.

Thou with sinners wont to eat,
Who with loving words didst greet
Mary weeping at Thy feet;
Hear us, Holy JESU.

Thou Who by a look didst chide
Peter when, by Satan tried,
Thee His LORD he thrice denied;
Hear us, Holy JESU.

Thou by Jewish hate refused,
And for man's transgressions bruised,
Sinless, yet of sin accused;
Hear us, Holy JESU.

Thou Who, hanging on the Tree,
To the thief saidst, "Thou shalt be
To-day in Paradise with Me;"
Hear us, Holy JESU.

Thou Who on the Cross didst reign,
Dying there in bitter pain,
Cleansing us from sin's dark stain;
Hear us, Holy JESU.

Thou Whose will it is that we
Should from death return to Thee,
And should live eternally;
Hear us, Holy JESU.

II

SHEPHERD of the straying sheep,
Comforter of them that weep,
Crying to Thee from the deep;
Save us, Holy JESU.

In all poverty and wealth,
In all sickness and in health,
Ever from the tempter's stealth,
Save us, Holy JESU.

When the hour of death draws nigh,
When we hear the midnight cry,
Fount of pity, Judge most high;
Save us, Holy JESU.

That by truest penitence
We may cleanse our soul's offence,
Clothed by Thee with innocence,
Hear us, we beseech Thee.

That we give to sin no place,
That we never quench Thy grace,
That we alway seek Thy face,
Hear us, we beseech Thee.

That denying evil lust,
Living godly, meek, and just,
In Thy mercy we may trust,
Hear us, we beseech Thee.

That to sin for ever dead,
We may live to Thee instead,
And the narrow pathway tread,
Hear us, we beseech Thee.

When shall end the battle sore,
When our pilgrimage is o'er,
Grant us peace for evermore;
Hear us, we beseech Thee.

Verse—Second Tune
Response

II

SHEPHERD of the straying sheep,
Comforter of them that weep,
Crying to Thee from the deep;
Save us, Holy Jesu.

In all poverty and wealth,
In all sickness and in health,
Ever from the tempter's stealth,
Save us, Holy Jesu.

When the hour of death draws nigh,
When we hear the midnight cry,
Fount of pity, Judge most high;
Save us, Holy Jesu.

That by truest penitence
We may cleanse our soul's offence,
Clothed by Thee with innocence,
Hear us, we beseech Thee.

That we give to sin no place,
That we never quench Thy grace,
That we alway seek Thy face,
Hear us, we beseech Thee.

That denying evil lust,
Living godly, meek, and just,
In Thy mercy we may trust,
Hear us, we beseech Thee.

That to sin for ever dead,
We may live to Thee instead,
And the narrow pathway tread,
Hear us, we beseech Thee.

When shall end the battle sore,
When our pilgrimage is o'er,
Grant us peace for evermore;
Hear us, we beseech Thee.

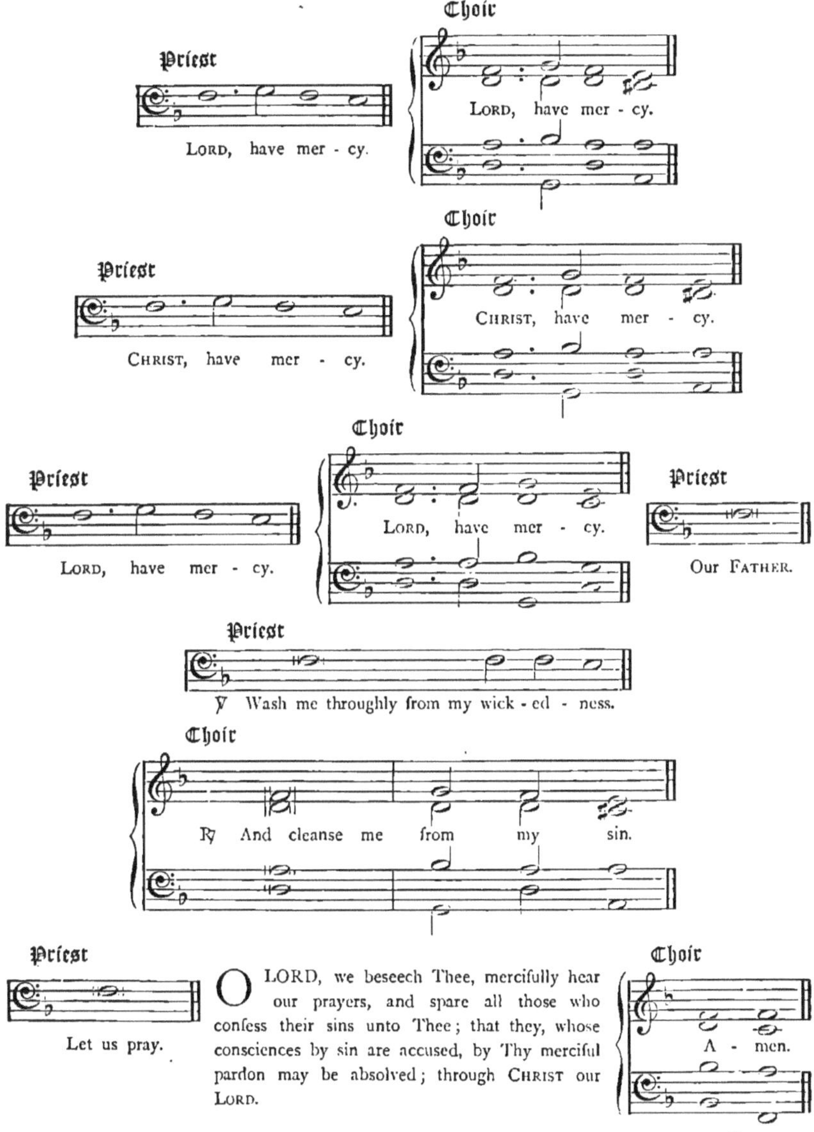
Priest
LORD, have mer - cy.
Choir
LORD, have mer - cy.
Priest
CHRIST, have mer - cy.
Choir
CHRIST, have mer - cy.
Priest
LORD, have mer - cy.
Choir
LORD, have mer - cy.
Priest
Our FATHER.
Priest
℣ Wash me throughly from my wick - ed - ness.
Choir
℟ And cleanse me from my sin.
Priest
Let us pray.
Choir
A - men.

O LORD, we beseech Thee, mercifully hear our prayers, and spare all those who confess their sins unto Thee; that they, whose consciences by sin are accused, by Thy merciful pardon may be absolved; through CHRIST our LORD.

LITANY OF THE PASSION—No. I

Choir
Priest or Two Cantors
LORD, have mer - cy.
LORD, have mer - cy.
Choir
Priest
CHRIST, have . . mer - - cy.
CHRIST, have mer - cy.
Choir
Priest
LORD, have . . mer - cy.
LORD, have mer - cy.
Verse—FIRST TUNE
Response

LORD, have mercy.
CHRIST, have mercy.
LORD, have mercy.

FATHER, Who gavest Thy SON to redeem us,
SAVIOUR, for us on the Cross Who didst die,
SPIRIT, Who crownest the work of redemption;
Hear us, we pray Thee, Good LORD.

WORD Everlasting, Incarnate of Mary,
Child in the manger, and GOD on the throne,
Humbled for us to the form of a servant;
Hear us, we pray Thee, Good LORD.

SAVIOUR most Mighty, in Calvary's conflict,
Girt with the sword of Goliath the strong,
Breaking the power of death by Thy dying;
Hear us, we pray Thee, Good LORD.

I

CHRIST with desire that Passover keeping,
Ere the true Lamb once for all should be slain,
Sacrifice offered for all and for ever;
Hear us, we pray Thee, Good LORD.

JESU, alone with the blood sweat upon Thee,
JESU, in agony bowed to the earth,
JESU, Thy will to the FATHER resigning;
Hear us, we pray Thee, Good LORD.

JESU, betrayed by the kiss of the traitor,
Bound by the cords which Thy creatures entwined,
Bound by Thy love yet more strongly and surely;
Hear us, we pray Thee, Good LORD.

JESU, from Annas to Caiaphas hurried,
Blindfolded, stricken, and falsely accused,
Rudely blasphemed and declared a blasphemer;
Hear us, we pray Thee, Good LORD.

JESU, denied by Thy zealous Apostle,
Whom with a look Thou didst straightway recall,
Moving him sweetly to tears and contrition;
Hear us, we pray Thee, Good LORD.

Outraged and mocked by the soldiers of Herod,
Standing alone in the midst of the hall,
Thou Who couldst summon twelve legions of Angels;
Hear us, we pray Thee, Good LORD.

JESU, led forth to the clamouring people,
Maddened by hatred Barabbas to choose,
Thee the most Holy and Just One rejecting;
Hear us, we pray Thee, Good LORD.

Crowned with the wreath of Thy virgin espousals,
Woven of thorns, with the blood-crimsoned points,
Now with the crowns of Thy glory resplendent;
Hear us, we pray Thee, Good LORD.

Thou Who wast wounded to heal our transgressions,
Lifted on high to draw all men to Thee,
Mightily bruising the head of the serpent;
Hear us, we pray Thee, Good LORD.

Rending the veil of the Temple asunder,
By the centurion straightway adored,
Owned by the earthquake in darkness and terror;
Hear us, we pray Thee, Good LORD.

JESU, a bone of Whom should not be broken,
JESU, Whose side was pierced through with a spear;
Whence flowed the Blood and the Water of healing;
Hear us, we pray Thee, Good LORD.

Verse—Second Tune
Response

II

O BY the chastisement cruel and bloody,
Which for our peace from the scourge Thou didst bear,
That by Thy stripes all our sins may be healed;
Hear us, we pray Thee, Good LORD.

O by the title set up in derision,
"JESUS of Nazareth, King of the Jews,"
Telling it out from the Tree that Thou reignest;
Hear us, we pray Thee, Good LORD.

By the dear Name of Thy dread incarnation
Name of salvation that saves us from sin,
High over all things, the sweet Name of JESUS;
Hear us, we pray Thee, Good LORD.

By Thy five Wounds, each a porch of Bethesda,
Whither the impotent alway resort,
Finding their strength in the Fountain of mercy;
Hear us, we pray Thee, Good LORD,

By the Oblation of holy remembrance,
When with the FATHER Thy merits we plead,
Kneeling before Thee in lowliest worship;
Hear us, we pray Thee, Good LORD.

LORD, by the Presence we hail at Thine Altar,
True GOD and Man, both the Victim and Priest,
Where we adore Thee revealed and yet hidden;
Hear us, we pray Thee, Good LORD.

JESU, Immaculate Lamb without blemish,
Taking away all the sins of the world,
By Thine one Offering perfect for ever;
Hear us, we pray Thee, Good LORD.

III

JESU, the Cross-bearer going before us,
Teaching us also to follow Thy steps,
That we may bear what Thou layest upon us,
Hear us, we pray Thee, Good LORD.

Thou Whose long-suffering goodness was waiting
While our dull hearts were unmoved at Thy call;
That in repentance we may be forgiven,
Hear us, we pray Thee, Good LORD.

That, being cleansed from our sins and transgressions,
We may beware lest we put Thee to shame,
Wilfully sinning away our salvation,
Hear us, we pray Thee, Good LORD.

Freed from the enemy's chains which had bound us,
Walking from henceforth in newness of life,
That we may faithfully serve and adore Thee,
Hear us, we pray Thee, Good LORD.

Priest
LORD, have mer - cy.
Choir
LORD, have mer - cy.
Priest
CHRIST, have mer - cy.
Choir
CHRIST, have mer - cy.
Priest
LORD, have mer - cy.
Choir
LORD, have mer - cy.
Priest
Our FATHER.
Priest
℣ Thou wast slain.
Choir
℟ And hast re - deem - ed us to GOD.
Priest
Let us pray.
Choir
A - men.

ALMIGHTY and Everlasting GOD, Who of Thy tender love towards mankind, hast sent Thy SON our SAVIOUR JESUS CHRIST, to take upon Him our flesh, and to suffer death upon the Cross, that all mankind should follow the example of His great humility; mercifully grant, that we may both follow the example of His patience, and also be made partakers of His resurrection; through the Same JESUS CHRIST our LORD.

LITANY OF THE PASSION—No. II

Priest or Two Cantors
Lord, have mer - cy.
Choir
dim.
Lord, have mer - cy.
Priest
cres.
Christ, have mer - cy.
Choir
cres.
Christ, have mer - cy.
Priest
Slower
pp
Lord, have mer - cy.
Choir
Slow
pp
Lord, have mer - cy.
Verse—First Tune
Response

LORD, have mercy.
CHRIST, have mercy.
LORD, have mercy.

GOD the FATHER, GOD the SON,
GOD the SPIRIT, Three in One,
In the hope of pardon won;
Hear us, Holy TRINITY.

JESU, born to grief and pain,
That redeemed from sin's dark stain
Life eternal we might gain;
Hear us, Holy JESU.

JESU, born to set us free,
Who for thirty years and three
Didst on earth vouchsafe to be;
Hear us, Holy JESU.

JESU, Who didst testify,
When Thine hour was drawing nigh,
How the SON of Man must die;
Hear us, Holy JESU.

JESU, Who in that sad week,
Mild and Awful, Just and Meek,
Didst Thy last dread warnings speak;
Hear us, Holy JESU.

JESU, Who didst fully know
Every pang of direst woe,
Which Thy soul must undergo;
Hear us, Holy JESU.

JESU, Who Thy Flesh and Blood
Gavest first to be our food,
Then our ransom on the Rood;
Hear us, Holy JESU.

JESU, in Gethsemane
Bowed in sweat of blood, that we
Might from sin redeemed be;
Hear us, Holy JESU.

JESU, by Thy friend betrayed;
JESU, sport for sinners made;
JESU, in mock robes arrayed;
Hear us, Holy JESU.

JESU, Whom the soldiers crowned
With sharp thorns Thy brow around,
And Thy hands most holy bound;
Hear us, Holy JESU.

JESU, Whom condemned to die,
Scourged and stripped in agony,
Wicked men did crucify;
Hear us, Holy JESU

JESU, reigning from the Tree,
Lifted up on Calvary,
Drawing all men unto Thee;
Hear us, Holy JESU

JESU, Who didst utter there
Words of power and of prayer,
Triumph high and tender care;
Hear us, Holy JESU

JESU, by the precious flood
Of Thy all redeeming blood,
Reconciling us to GOD;
Hear us, Holy JESU.

By Thy Body rent and torn,
By Thy Soul oppressed with scorn,
By Thy Pains so meekly borne;
Save us, Holy JESU.

By Thy Willingness to die,
By Thy loud and bitter Cry,
By Thy last expiring Sigh;
Save us, Holy JESU.

That Thy love may grant that we
May be wholly drawn to Thee,
Lifted on the shameful Tree,
Hear us, we beseech Thee.

That the Blood, which Thou in pain
Shedd'st for our eternal gain,
May not have been shed in vain,
Hear us, we beseech Thee

That we, learning more and more
Of Thy Death and Passion sore,
For Thy love may Thee adore,
Hear us, we beseech Thee.

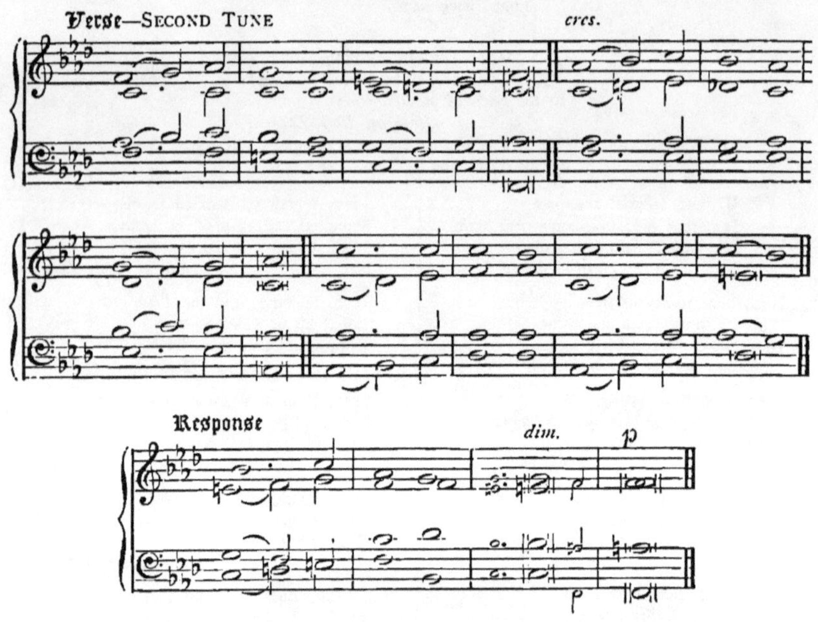
Verse—Second Tune
cres.
Response
dim.
p

BY Thy Body rent and torn,
By Thy Soul oppressed with scorn,
By Thy Pains so meekly borne;
Save us, Holy Jesu.

By Thy Willingness to die,
By Thy loud and bitter Cry,
By Thy last expiring Sigh;
Save us, Holy Jesu.

That Thy love may grant that we
May be wholly drawn to Thee,
Lifted on the shameful Tree,
Hear us, we beseech Thee.

That the Blood, which Thou in pain
Shedd'st for our eternal gain,
May not have been shed in vain,
Hear us, we beseech Thee.

That we, learning more and more
Of Thy Death and Passion sore,
For Thy love may Thee adore,
Hear us, we beseech Thee.

Priest
Lord, have mer - cy.
Choir
p
dim.
Lord, have mer - cy.
Priest
cres.
Christ, have mer - cy.
Choir
cres.
Christ, have mer - cy.
Priest
Slower
pp
Lord, have mer - cy.
Choir
Slow
pp
Lord, have mer - cy.
Priest
Our Father.
Priest
℣ The chastisement of our peace was up - on Him.
Choir
p
℟ And with His stripes we are heal - ed.
Priest
Let us pray.
Choir
A - men.

ALMIGHTY GOD, we beseech Thee graciously to behold this Thy family, for which our Lord Jesus Christ was contented to be betrayed, and given up into the hands of wicked men, and to suffer death upon the Cross, Who now liveth and reigneth with Thee and the Holy Ghost, ever One God, world without end.

Easter

LITANY OF THE RESURRECTION

Priest or Two Cantors
Lord, have mer - cy.
Choir
Lord, have mer - cy.
Priest
Christ, have mer-cy.
Choir
Christ, have mer-cy.
Priest
Lord, have mer-cy.
Choir
rall.
Lord, have mer - cy.
Verse—First Tune
Response

God the Father, God the Son,
God the Spirit, Three in One,
In our joy for victory won;
Hear us, Holy Trinity.

Christ, on Whom our sins were laid,
Who for us the price hast paid,
Paschal Lamb, true Offering made;
Hear us, Holy Jesu.

Who by dying death hast slain,
Who from death art risen again,
Lord o'er heaven and earth to reign;
Hear us, Holy Jesu.

Verse—Second Tune

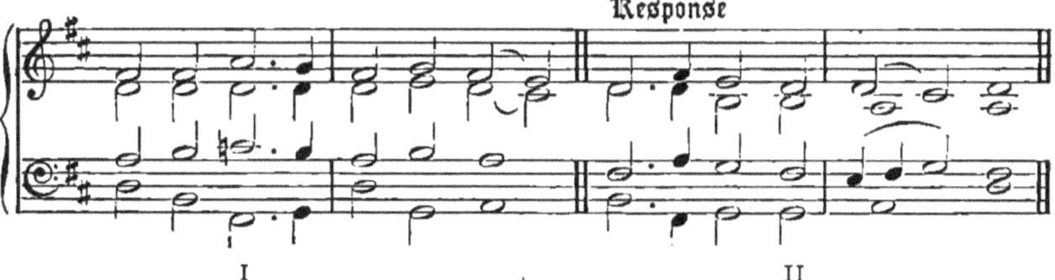
Response

I

WHO the dragon wounding sore,
Didst unbar the brazen door,
Opening it for evermore;
Hear us, Holy Jesu.

Thou Who didst Thy message tell
Unto these who sometime fell,
Spirits bound in courts of hell;
Hear us, Holy Jesu.

Who across the parted flood,
Through the Red Sea of Thy Blood
Mad'st a pathway unto God;
Hear us, Holy Jesu.

Who didst exultation shed
On the hearts whence joy had fled,
First-begotten from the dead;
Hear us, Holy Jesu.

Who didst rise ere yet the night
On that Easter morning bright
Fled before the dawning light;
Hear us, Holy Jesu.

Thou Whose Angels came to tell
To the few who loved Thee well
How their Lord had conquered hell;
Hear us, Holy Jesu.

Who by Mary Magdalene,
From her sevenfold sin made clean,
First in glorious form wast seen;
Hear us, Holy Jesu.

Who with loving words didst greet
Those who brought the spices sweet,
Worshipping at Thy dear feet;
Hear us, Holy Jesu.

II

WHO, discoursing by the way,
Didst the mysteries display
That within the Scriptures lay;
Hear us, Holy Jesu.

Who at Emmaus didst abide,
One short hour, at even-tide,
Known at last, the Crucified;
Hear us, Holy Jesu.

Thou Whose wounds all doubt o'ercame,
Thou Whose words of gentle blame
Filled the doubter's heart with shame;
Hear us, Holy Jesu.

Who didst meet Thine own once more
In the morning on the shore,
Feeding them from mystic store;
Hear us, Holy Jesu.

Thou Who Peter, sorrowing deep,
Thrice didst bid Thy flock to keep,
"Feed My lambs" and "feed My sheep;"
Hear us, Holy Jesu.

Who didst bless Thy chosen band,
Princes sent to every land,
With the might of Thy right hand;
Hear us, Holy Jesu.

Thou Whose risen power is shewn
Wheresoe'er Thy Name is known,
Interceding at the throne;
Hear us, Holy Jesu.

Thou by Whose undying care,
Mortals who Thy Priesthood share
To their brethren pardon bear;
Hear us, Holy Jesu.

Verse—Third Tune

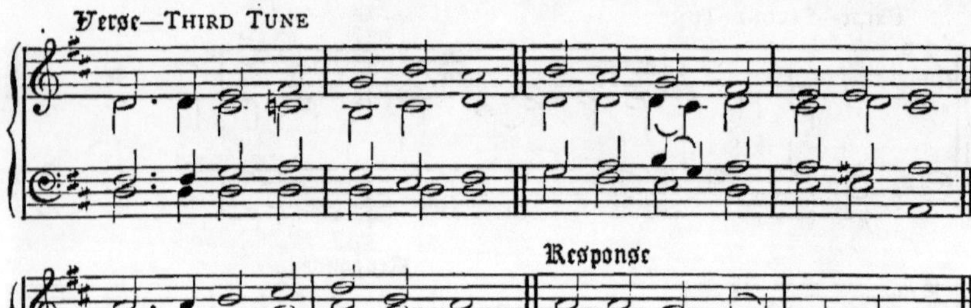

Response

II

WHO, discoursing by the way,
Didst the mysteries display
That within the Scriptures lay;
Hear us, Holy Jesu.

Who at Emmaus didst abide,
One short hour, at even-tide,
Known at last, the Crucified;
Hear us, Holy Jesu.

Thou Whose wounds all doubt o'ercame,
Thou Whose words of gentle blame
Filled the doubter's heart with shame;
Hear us, Holy Jesu.

Who didst meet Thine own once more
In the morning on the shore,
Feeding them from mystic store;
Hear us, Holy Jesu.

Thou Who Peter, sorrowing deep,
Thrice didst bid Thy flock to keep,
"Feed My lambs" and "feed My sheep;"
Hear us, Holy Jesu.

Who didst bless Thy chosen band,
Princes sent to every land,
With the might of Thy right hand;
Hear us, Holy Jesu.

Thou Whose risen power is shewn
Wheresoe'er Thy name is known,
Interceding at the throne;
Hear us, Holy Jesu.

Thou by Whose undying care,
Mortals who Thy Priesthood share
To their brethren pardon bear;
Hear us, Holy Jesu.

III

THAT from Satan's power set free,
Dead to sin and vanity,
We may henceforth rise with Thee,
Hear us, we beseech Thee.

That in risen life we strive,
By the power which Thou dost give,
Evermore in Thee to live,
Hear us, we beseech Thee.

That upon our dying bed
Thou wouldst grace and comfort shed,
Lord of living and of dead,
Hear us, we beseech Thee.

That when death shall seal our eyes,
Light may on our pathway rise
Guiding us to Paradise,
Hear us, we beseech Thee

That within the better land
We, with all the patient band
Of Thy waiting Saints, may stand,
Hear us, we beseech Thee.

That when through the earth and sky
Rings the Archangel's voice on high
We may hail Thee drawing nigh,
Hear us, we beseech Thee.

That Thy face we may not fear,
But Thy words of welcome dear,
"Come, ye blessed," we may hear,
Hear us, we beseech Thee.

That our bodies then may shine,
Changed and glorified with Thine,
Radiant in the light divine,
Hear us, we beseech Thee.

That for all eternity
By Thy Rising we may be
Bound in perfect love to Thee,
Hear us, we beseech Thee.

Priest
LORD, have mer - cy.
Choir
LORD, have mer - cy.
Priest
CHRIST, have mer - cy.
Choir
CHRIST, have mer - cy.
Priest
LORD, have mer - cy.
Choir
rall.
LORD, have mer - cy.
Priest
Our FATHER.
Priest
℣ The Right Hand of the LORD hath the pre - em - in - ence.
Choir
℟ The Right Hand of the LORD bringeth migh - ty things to pass.
Priest
Let us pray.
Choir
A - men.

ALMIGHTY GOD, Who through Thine Only-begotten SON JESUS CHRIST hast overcome death, and opened unto us the gate of everlasting life; we humbly beseech Thee, that, as by Thy special grace preventing us, Thou dost put into our minds good desires, so by Thy continual help we may bring the same to good effect; through JESUS CHRIST our LORD, Who liveth and reigneth with Thee and the HOLY GHOST, ever One GOD, world without end.

LITANY FOR ROGATION DAYS

Priest or Two Cantors
LORD, have mer - cy.
Choir
LORD, have mer - cy.
Priest
CHRIST, have mer - cy.
Choir
CHRIST, have mer - - cy.
Priest
LORD, have mer - cy.
Choir
LORD, have mer - cy.
Verse—FIRST TUNE
Response

LORD, have mercy.
CHRIST, have mercy.
LORD, have mercy.

GOD the FATHER, GOD the SON,
GOD the SPIRIT, ever One,
While eternal ages run;
Hear us, Holy TRINITY.

Thou the GOD Who hearest prayer,
Thou Who mak'st our wants Thy care,
Thou Who dost in mercy spare;
Hear us, Holy JESU.

Thou by Whom the dews are shed,
By Whose hand the birds are fed,
Giver of our daily bread;
Hear us, Holy JESU.

Thou Who didst with power benign
To Thy Mother's prayer incline,
Changing water into wine;
Hear us, Holy JESU.

Thou Who in the wilderness
Slender store didst richly bless,
Feeding thousands in distress;
Hear us, Holy JESU.

Thou Whose care Thy creatures shew,
Lilies that untoiling grow,
All things lovely here below;
Hear us, Holy JESU.

In the fruitful time of mirth,
In the hour of cruel dearth,
Thou the Hope of all the earth;
Hear us, we beseech Thee.

That entrusted by Thy love
With Thy gifts from Heaven above,
Faithful stewards we may prove,
Hear us, we beseech Thee.

That the earth may yield her seed,
Giving man in every need
Wine to gladden, bread to feed,
Hear us, we beseech Thee.

That Thy gifts of healthful air,
Genial warmth, and seasons fair,
May Thy gracious power declare,
Hear us, we beseech Thee.

That, whate'er our blessings be,
We with thankful hearts may see
Thee in all, and all from Thee,
Hear us, we beseech Thee.

That when all our care is past,
Ended vigil, strife, and fast,
We may win the crown at last,
Hear us, we beseech Thee.

Verse—SECOND TUNE

Response

GOD the FATHER, GOD the SON,
GOD the SPIRIT, ever One,
While eternal ages run;
Hear us, Holy TRINITY.

Thou the GOD Who hearest prayer,
Thou Who mak'st our wants Thy care,
Thou Who dost in mercy spare;
Hear us, Holy JESU.

Thou by Whom the dews are shed,
By Whose hand the birds are fed,
Giver of our daily bread;
Hear us, Holy JESU.

Thou Who didst with power benign
To Thy Mother's prayer incline,
Changing water into wine;
Hear us, Holy JESU.

Thou Who in the wilderness
Slender store didst richly bless,
Feeding thousands in distress;
Hear us, Holy JESU.

Thou Whose care Thy creatures shew,
Lilies that untoiling grow,
All things lovely here below;
Hear us, Holy JESU.

In the fruitful time of mirth,
In the hour of cruel dearth,
Thou the Hope of all the earth;
Hear us, we beseech Thee.

That entrusted by Thy love
With Thy gifts from Heaven above,
Faithful stewards we may prove,
Hear us, we beseech Thee.

That the earth may yield her seed,
Giving man in every need
Wine to gladden, bread to feed,
Hear us, we beseech Thee.

That Thy gifts of healthful air,
Genial warmth, and seasons fair,
May Thy gracious power declare,
Hear us, we beseech Thee.

That, whate'er our blessings be,
We with thankful hearts may see
Thee in all, and all from Thee,
Hear us, we beseech Thee.

That when all our care is past,
Ended vigil, strife, and fast,
We may win the crown at last,
Hear us, we beseech Thee.

Priest
LORD, have mer - cy.
Choir
LORD, have mer - cy.
Priest
CHRIST, have mer - cy.
Choir
CHRIST, have mer - cy.
Priest
LORD, have mer - cy.
Choir
LORD, have mer - cy.
Priest
Our FATHER.
Priest
℣ In the evening, and morning, and at noontide will I pray, and that in - stant - ly.
Choir
℟ And He shall hear my voice.
Priest
Let us pray.

O GOD, our Refuge and Strength, Who art the Author of all godliness; be ready, we beseech Thee, to hear the devout prayers of Thy Church; and grant that those things which we ask faithfully we may obtain effectually; through JESUS CHRIST our LORD.

Choir

A - men.

F

Ascension Tide

LITANY OF THE ASCENSION

Choir
Priest or Two Cantors
Lord, have mer - cy.
Lord, have . . mer - cy.
Choir
Priest
Christ, have mer - cy.
Christ, have . . mer - cy.
Choir
Priest
Lord, have mer - cy.
Lord, have . . mer - cy.
Verse—First Tune
Response

LORD have mercy.
CHRIST, have mercy.
LORD, have mercy.

GOD the FATHER, GOD the SON
High enthroned, the battle done,
GOD the SPIRIT, Three in One;
Hear us, Holy TRINITY.

JESU, Who to Bethany
Leddest forth once more with Thee
Those who should Thy glory see;
Hear us, Holy JESU.

Thou Who didst unto the end
Love and bless each chosen friend,
And while blessing didst ascend;
Hear us, Holy JESU.

I

WHO ascending up on high
To Thy throne above the sky,
Captive ledd'st captivity;
Hear us, Holy JESU.

Who didst victory achieve,
Opening heaven to receive
All who should in Thee believe;
Hear us, Holy JESU.

Who receivedst gifts of grace,
That with man's rebellious race
GOD might here have dwelling-place;
Hear us, Holy JESU.

Thou on Whom Thy GOD and LORD
Oil of gladness hath outpoured,
GOD in equal might adored;
Hear us, Holy JESU.

Thou on Whom in royal state
Angel hosts triumphant wait,
Opening wide the eternal gate;
Hear us, Holy JESU.

II

THOU Who midst the heavenly band,
Evermore at GOD'S right hand
Now to plead for us dost stand;
Hear us, Holy JESU.

Who to Heaven ascended, there
Dost a place for us prepare,
That Thy glory we may share;
Hear us, Holy JESU.

Who wilt come our Judge to be,
Bringing them that sleep in Thee,
Setting all Thy prisoners free;
Hear us, Holy JESU.

Thou through Whom all blessings flow,
Showering down on us below
Healing for our sin and woe;
Hear us, Holy JESU.

III

THAT Thy SPIRIT plenteously
May within us dwell, that we
Worthier temples prove for Thee,
Hear us, we beseech Thee.

That we walk henceforth aright,
Blameless in Thy holy sight,
Making Thee our one delight,
Hear us, we beseech Thee.

That in all our strife and fear
Thou our hearts wouldst stay and cheer,
Light in darkness ever near,
Hear us, we beseech Thee.

That from things of earth set free
Our uplifted hearts may be
Set on things above with Thee,
Hear us, we beseech Thee.

That Thy words we may obey,
That our footsteps may not stray,
Walking in the narrow way,
Hear us, we beseech Thee.

That the joy pledged to Thine own,
Though to this world all unknown,
May to us be richly shewn,
Hear us, we beseech Thee.

That when fails our earthly sight,
Faith may grasp with surer might,
Love may guide with clearer light,
Hear us, we beseech Thee.

That in living streams may flow
Plenteous grace on Saints below,
So Thy Church may live and grow,
Hear us, we beseech Thee.

That Thy Priests with righteousness,
And Thy Saints with joyfulness,
Out of Sion Thou wouldst bless,
Hear us, we beseech Thee.

That Thy servants waiting here
For Thy coming, SAVIOUR dear,
With Thy presence Thou wouldst cheer,
Hear us, we beseech Thee.

Till with awful, glad surprise,
Lifting up their longing eyes,
They behold Thee in the skies,
Hear us, we beseech Thee.

Verse—SECOND TUNE

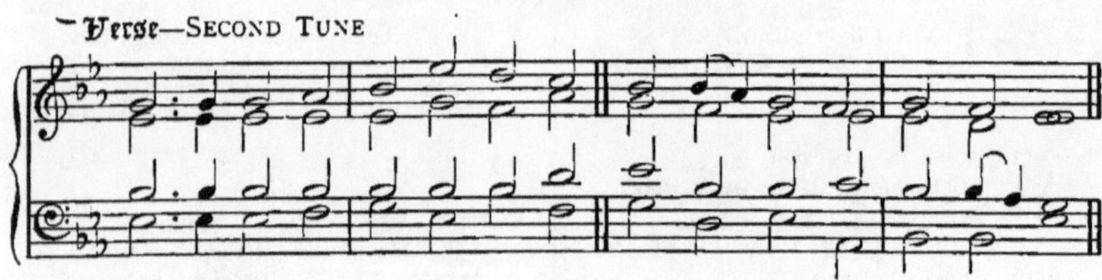

Response

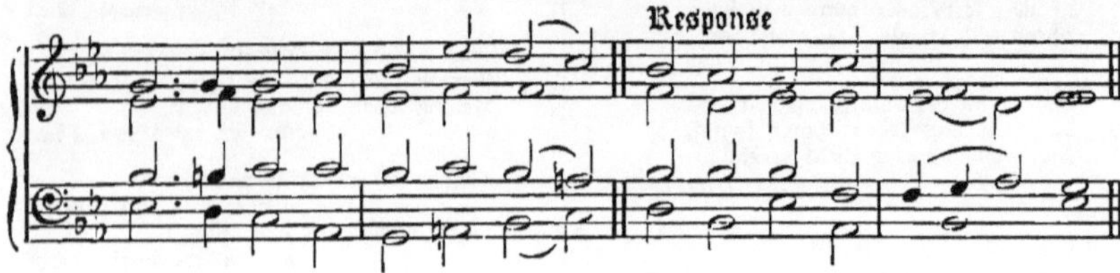

II

THOU Who midst the heavenly band,
Evermore at GOD's right hand,
Now to plead for us dost stand;
Hear us, Holy JESU.

Who to Heaven ascended, there
Dost a place for us prepare,
That Thy glory we may share;
Hear us, Holy JESU.

Who wilt come our Judge to be,
Bringing them that sleep in Thee,
Setting all Thy prisoners free;
Hear us, Holy JESU.

Thou through Whom all blessings flow,
Showering down on us below
Healing for our sin and woe;
Hear us, Holy JESU.

III

THAT Thy SPIRIT plenteously
May within us dwell, that we
Worthier temples prove for Thee,
Hear us, we beseech Thee.

That we walk henceforth aright,
Blameless in Thy holy sight,
Making Thee our one delight,
Hear us, we beseech Thee.

That in all our strife and fear
Thou our hearts wouldst stay and cheer,
Light in darkness ever near,
Hear us, we beseech Thee.

That from things of earth set free
Our uplifted hearts may be
Set on things above with Thee,
Hear us, we beseech Thee.

That Thy words we may obey,
That our footsteps may not stray,
Walking in the narrow way,
Hear us, we beseech Thee.

That the joy pledged to Thine own,
Though to this world all unknown,
May to us be richly shewn,
Hear us, we beseech Thee.

That when fails our earthly sight,
Faith may grasp with surer might,
Love may guide with clearer light,
Hear us, we beseech Thee.

That in living streams may flow
Plenteous grace on Saints below,
So Thy Church may live and grow,
Hear us, we beseech Thee.

That Thy Priests with righteousness,
And Thy Saints with joyfulness,
Out of Sion Thou wouldst bless,
Hear us, we beseech Thee.

That Thy servants waiting here
For Thy coming, SAVIOUR dear,
With Thy presence Thou wouldst cheer,
Hear us, we beseech Thee.

Till with awful, glad surprise,
Lifting up their longing eyes,
They behold Thee in the skies,
Hear us, we beseech Thee.

Priest
LORD, have mer - cy.
Choir
LORD, have . . mer - cy.
Priest
CHRIST, have mer - cy.
Choir
CHRIST, have . . mer - cy.
Priest
LORD, have mer - cy.
Choir
LORD, have . mer - cy.
Priest
Our FATHER.
Priest
℣ Thou art gone up on high.
Choir
℟ Thou hast led cap - tiv - i - ty cap - tive.
Priest
Let us pray.
Choir
A - men.

GRANT, we beseech Thee, Almighty GOD, that like as we do believe Thy Only begotten SON our LORD JESUS CHRIST to have ascended into the heavens; so we may also in heart and mind thither ascend, and with Him continually dwell, Who liveth and reigneth with Thee and the HOLY GHOST, One GOD, world without end.

Whitsuntide

LITANY OF THE HOLY GHOST—No. I

Choir
Priest
LORD, have mer - cy.
LORD, have mer - cy.
Choir
Priest
CHRIST, have mer-cy.
CHRIST, have mer-cy.
Priest
Choir
LORD, have mer-cy.
LORD, have mer - cy.
Verse—FIRST TUNE
Response
Slower
rall.
pp

LORD, have mercy.
CHRIST, have mercy.
LORD, have mercy.

FATHER, in heaven eternally reigning,
SON of the FATHER, Redeemer of men,
SPIRIT, amongst us for ever abiding;
Hear us, we pray Thee, Good LORD.

SPIRIT, adored over all things for ever,
One with the FATHER and One with the SON,
Life-giver, Holy and Loving Creator;
Hear us, we pray Thee, Good LORD.

Hallowing Breath of the FATHER Eternal,
Comforter, sent from the throne of our LORD,
GOD Who dost reign in Thy glory Co-equal;
Hear us, we pray Thee, Good LORD.

I

SPIRIT of Truth, Who didst speak by the Prophets
Signs to reveal of the SAVIOUR to come,
Ordering all in Thy manifold wisdom;
Hear us, we pray Thee, Good LORD.

SPIRIT of Life, overshadowing Mary,
That of a woman true GOD might be born,
Making incarnate the Word Everlasting,
Hear us, we pray Thee, Good LORD

SPIRIT, revealing to Saints in the Temple,
Him for Whose coming they waited so well,
Light of the Gentiles, and Israel's Glory;
Hear us, we pray Thee, Good LORD.

SPIRIT, on JESUS baptizèd in Jordan
Lighting from Heaven in form of a dove,
Sevenfold gifts on His manhood conferring;
Hear us, we pray Thee, Good LORD.

SPIRIT, by Whom He was led to the desert
All the assaults of His foe to repel,
That by Thy guidance we too may be victors;
Hear us, we pray Thee, Good LORD.

SPIRIT, through Whom, without spot our Redeemer
Offered Himself an Oblation to GOD,
Cleansed from dead works that ourselves we may offer;
Hear us, we pray Thee, Good LORD.

II

PROMISE shed forth by the love of the FATHER,
Gift of enlightenment, manifold Fire,
Filling the Church, and confirming the faithful;
Hear us, we pray Thee, Good LORD.

Blessed Restorer of union for all men,
Lost by the curse that on Babel once fell,
Teaching one truth by one voice to the nations;
Hear us, we pray Thee, Good LORD.

Wind of the LORD, by Whose breath on the waters
Melted and freed by the warmth of His Word,
Floods of salvation flowed forth in abundance;
Hear us, we pray Thee, Good LORD.

Life of the Sacraments, Whose operation
Gives them abundantly virtue and power,
That by Thy help we may rightly receive them,
Hear us, we pray Thee, Good LORD.

Thou Who dost work with the words and the water,
Thou Who conferrest the seal of the LORD,
Thou Who to penitents bring'st absolution;
Hear us, we pray Thee, Good LORD.

Thou by Whose power the Body of JESUS
Here at our altars is truly received,
And in Memorial Sacrifice offered;
Hear us, we pray Thee, Good LORD.

Verse—Second Tune
Response
Slower
pp

III

SPIRIT of Holiness, meetly dividing
Gifts to Thy faithful, for each and for all,
That Thou wouldst hallow our Bishops and Clergy,
Hear us, we pray Thee, Good Lord.

That they may rule by the grace of Thy wisdom,
Ever contend for the Truth in Thy might,
Boldly rebuke as Thy will shall direct them,
Hear us, we pray Thee, Good Lord.

That for the sake of the Lord Who doth choose them,
Earth and its pleasures their hearts may resign,
Nailed to His Cross, and conformed to His Passion,
Hear us, we pray Thee, Good Lord.

That they may learn to be all things to all men,
Servants to all, that the more they may gain,
Vessels appointed for life and salvation,
Hear us, we pray Thee, Good Lord.

IV

O THAT the fruits Thou dost bring to their fulness,
When to the flesh the affections have died,
May be shewn forth in the lives of Thy servants,
Hear us, we pray Thee, Good Lord.

When, like a flood, on the children of Jesus
Suddenly cometh the enemy's power,
That Thou wouldst raise up a standard against him,
Hear us, we pray Thee, Good Lord.

That Thou wouldst save us from slighting Thy presence,
Grieving Thy love, or refusing to hear
Where Thou dost speak in the depth of our conscience,
Hear us, we pray Thee, Good Lord.

That Thou wouldst hold us from pride and presumption,
That Thou wouldst shield us from doubt and despair,
And from the sin that can ne'er be forgiven,
Hear us, we pray Thee, Good Lord.

O that our hearts Thou wouldst purify wholly,
Leading us on to the sight of our God,
That we may love Him for ever and ever,
Hear us, we pray Thee, Good Lord.

Spirit most awful, that, as we adore Thee,
All our infirmities Thou wouldst forgive,
Pardon our ignorance, lighten our darkness,
Hear us, we pray Thee, Good Lord.

That in the day of the last separation
Thou wouldst receive us, and own us for Thine,
Pouring upon us Thy full benediction,
Hear us, we pray Thee, Good Lord.

Priest
LORD, have mer - cy.
Choir
LORD, have mer - cy.
Priest
CHRIST, have mer - cy.
Choir
CHRIST, have mer - cy.
Priest
LORD, have mer - cy.
Choir
LORD, have mer - cy.
Priest
Our FATHER.
Priest
℣ The COMFORTER, which is the HO - LY GHOST,
Choir
℟ Shall teach you all things.
Priest
Let us pray.

GOD, Who (as at this time) didst teach the hearts of Thy faithful people, by the sending to them the light of Thy HOLY SPIRIT; grant us by the Same SPIRIT to have a right judgment in all things, and evermore to rejoice in His holy comfort; through the merits of CHRIST JESUS our SAVIOUR, Who liveth and reigneth with Thee, in the unity of the Same SPIRIT, One GOD, world without end.

Choir
A - men.

LITANY OF THE HOLY GHOST—No. II

Priest or Two Cantors
LORD, have mer - cy.
Choir
LORD, have mer-cy.
Priest
CHRIST, have mer-cy.
Choir
CHRIST, have mer-cy.
Priest
LORD, have mer - cy.
Choir
LORD, have mer - - - cy.
— Verse—FIRST TUNE
Response

LORD, have mercy.
CHRIST, have mercy.
LORD, have mercy.

FATHER, in heaven eternally reigning,
SON of the FATHER, Redeemer of men,
SPIRIT, amongst us for ever abiding;
Hear us, we pray Thee, Good LORD.

SPIRIT, adored over all things for ever,
One with the FATHER and One with the SON,
Life-giver, Holy and Loving Creator;
Hear us, we pray Thee, Good LORD.

Hallowing BREATH of the FATHER Eternal,
COMFORTER, sent from the throne of our LORD,
GOD Who dost reign in Thy glory Co-equal;
Hear us, we pray Thee, Good LORD.

I

SPIRIT of Truth, Who didst speak by the Prophets
Signs to reveal of the SAVIOUR to come,
Ordering all in Thy manifold wisdom;
Hear us, we pray Thee, Good LORD.

SPIRIT of Life, overshadowing Mary,
That of a woman true GOD might be born,
Making incarnate the Word Everlasting,
Hear us, we pray Thee, Good LORD.

SPIRIT, revealing to Saints in the Temple,
Him for Whose coming they waited so well,
Light of the Gentiles, and Israel's Glory;
Hear us, we pray Thee, Good LORD.

SPIRIT, on JESUS baptizèd in Jordan
Lighting from heaven in form of a dove,
Sevenfold gifts on His manhood conferring;
Hear us, we pray Thee, Good LORD.

SPIRIT, by Whom He was led to the desert
All the assaults of His foe to repel,
That by Thy guidance we too may be victors;
Hear us, we pray Thee, Good LORD.

SPIRIT, through Whom, without spot our Redeemer
Offered Himself an Oblation to GOD,
Cleansed from dead works that ourselves we may offer;
Hear us, we pray Thee, Good LORD.

II

PROMISE shed forth by the love of the FATHER,
Gift of enlightenment, manifold Fire,
Filling the Church, and confirming the faithful;
Hear us, we pray Thee, Good LORD

Blessed Restorer of union for all men,
Lost by the curse that on Babel once fell,
Teaching one truth by one voice to the nations;
Hear us, we pray Thee, Good LORD.

Wind of the LORD, by Whose breath on the waters
Melted and freed by the warmth of His Word,
Floods of salvation flowed forth in abundance;
Hear us, we pray Thee, Good LORD.

Life of the Sacraments, Whose operation
Gives them abundantly virtue and power,
That by Thy help we may rightly receive them,
Hear us, we pray Thee, Good LORD.

Thou Who dost work with the words and the water,
Thou Who conferrest the seal of the LORD,
Thou Who to penitents bring'st absolution;
Hear us, we pray Thee, Good LORD.

Thou by Whose power the Body of JESUS
Here at our altars is truly received,
And in Memorial Sacrifice offered;
Hear us, we pray Thee, Good LORD.

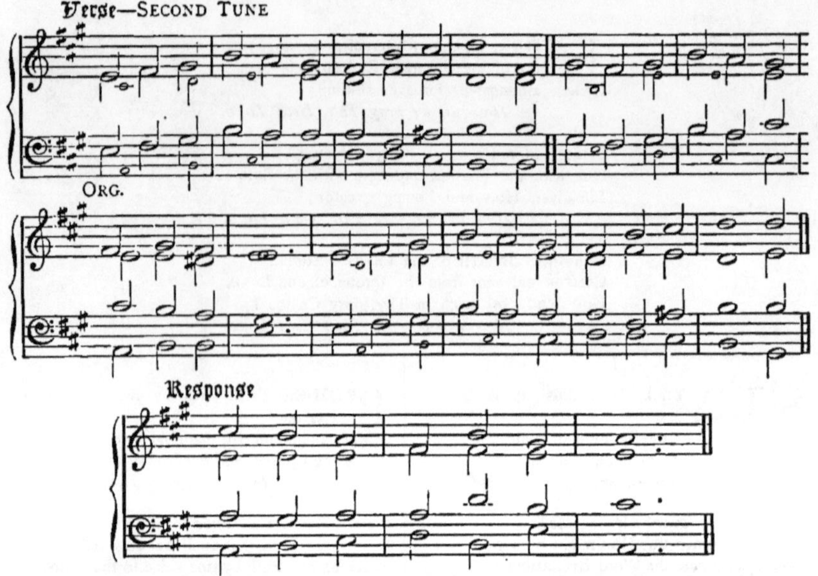
Verse—Second Tune
Org.
Response

III

SPIRIT of Holiness, meetly dividing
Gifts to Thy faithful, for each and for all,
That Thou wouldst hallow our Bishops and Clergy,
Hear us, we pray Thee, Good Lord.

That they may rule by the grace of Thy wisdom,
Ever contend for the Truth in Thy might,
Boldly rebuke as Thy will shall direct them,
Hear us, we pray Thee, Good Lord.

That for the sake of the Lord Who doth choose them,
Earth and its pleasures their hearts may resign,
Nailed to His Cross, and conformed to His Passion,
Hear us, we pray Thee, Good Lord.

That they may learn to be all things to all men,
Servants to all, that the more they may gain,
Vessels appointed for life and salvation,
Hear us, we pray Thee, Good Lord.

IV

O THAT the fruits Thou dost bring to their fulness,
When to the flesh the affections have died,
May be shewn forth in the lives of Thy servants,
Hear us, we pray Thee, Good Lord.

When, like a flood, on the children of Jesus
Suddenly cometh the enemy's power,
That Thou wouldst raise up a standard against him,
Hear us, we pray Thee, Good Lord.

That Thou wouldst save us from slighting Thy presence,
Grieving Thy love, or refusing to hear
Where Thou dost speak in the depth of our conscience,
Hear us, we pray Thee, Good Lord.

That Thou wouldst hold us from pride and presumption,
That Thou wouldst shield us from doubt and despair,
And from the sin that can ne'er be forgiven,
Hear us, we pray Thee, Good Lord.

O that our hearts Thou wouldst purify wholly,
Leading us on to the sight of our God,
That we may love Him for ever and ever,
Hear us, we pray Thee, Good Lord.

Spirit most awful, that, as we adore Thee,
All our infirmities Thou wouldst forgive,
Pardon our ignorance, lighten our darkness,
Hear us, we pray Thee, Good Lord.

That in the day of the last separation,
Thou wouldst receive us, and own us for Thine,
Pouring upon us Thy full benediction,
Hear us, we pray Thee, Good Lord.

Priest
LORD, have mer - cy.
Choir
LORD, have mer - cy.
Priest
CHRIST, have mer - cy.
Choir
CHRIST, have mer - cy.
Priest
LORD, have mer - cy.
Choir
LORD, have mer - - - - cy.
Priest
Our FATHER.
Priest
℣ The COMFORTER, which is the HO - LY GHOST,
Choir
℟ Shall teach you all . . things.
Priest
Let us pray.
Choir
A . . men.

GOD, Who (as at this time) didst teach the hearts of Thy faithful people, by the sending to them the light of Thy HOLY SPIRIT; grant us by the Same SPIRIT to have a right judgment in all things, and evermore to rejoice in His holy comfort; through the merits of CHRIST JESUS our SAVIOUR, Who liveth and reigneth with Thee, in the unity of the Same SPIRIT, One GOD, world without end.

LITANY OF THE HOLY GHOST—No. III

Choir
Priest or Two Cantors
LORD, have mercy.
LORD, have mercy.
Choir
Priest
CHRIST, have mercy.
CHRIST, have mercy.
Choir
rall.
Priest
LORD, have mer - cy.
LORD, have mercy.
Verse—FIRST TUNE
Response

LORD, have mercy.
CHRIST, have mercy.
LORD, have mercy.

GOD the FATHER, GOD the WORD,
GOD the HOLY GHOST adored,
Blessed TRINITY, One LORD;
Hear us, Holy TRINITY.

HOLY SPIRIT, heavenly Dove,
Dew descending from above,
Breath of life, and Fire of love;
Hear us, HOLY SPIRIT.

Thou by Whom a Virgin bore
Him Whom Heaven and earth adore,
Sent our nature to restore;
Hear us, HOLY SPIRIT.

Thou Whom JESUS from His throne
Gave to cheer and help His own,
That they might not be alone;
Hear us, HOLY SPIRIT.

SPIRIT, guarding us from ill,
Bending right our stubborn will,
Though we grieve Thee, patient
Hear us, HOLY SPIRIT.

SPIRIT, strength of all the weak,
Giving courage to the meek,
Teaching faltering tongues to speak;
Hear us, HOLY SPIRIT.

SPIRIT, aiding all who yearn
More of truth divine to learn,
And with deeper love to burn;
Hear us, HOLY SPIRIT.

SPIRIT, Whom by sin we grieve,
Whom the world will not receive,
Who dost help us to believe;
Hear us, HOLY SPIRIT.

Thou Who, when by sin we fall,
And when snares our souls enthral,
Lead'st us back with gentle call;
Hear us, HOLY SPIRIT.

That Thou wouldst Thy gifts bestow,
Gifts of wisdom GOD to know,
Gifts of strength to meet the foe,
Hear us, we beseech Thee.

That to sin we may be dead,
And by Thee in meekness led
May the narrow pathway tread,
Hear us, we beseech Thee.

That whene'er we go astray,
Thine illuminating ray
Guide us to the truer way,
Hear us, we beseech Thee.

That we alway live to Thee
In all grace and purity,
Thine, for ever Thine, to be,
Hear us, we beseech Thee.

That all-holy as Thou art,
Thou wouldst dwell within our heart,
Never from us to depart,
Hear us, we beseech Thee.

Verse—SECOND TUNE

Response

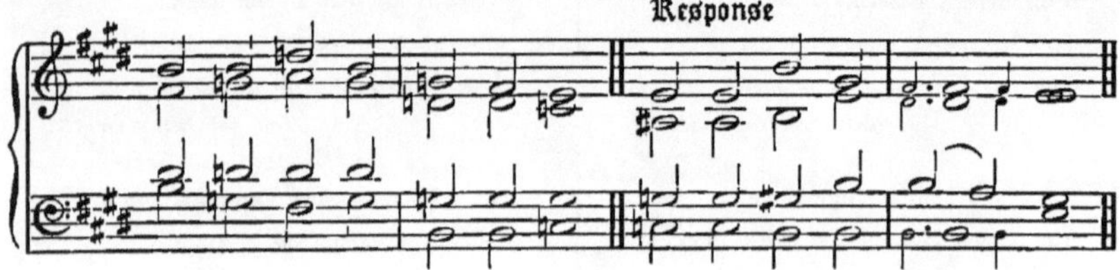

GOD the FATHER, God the WORD,
God the HOLY GHOST adored,
Blessed TRINITY, One LORD;
Hear us, Holy TRINITY.

HOLY SPIRIT, heavenly Dove,
Dew descending from above,
Breath of life, and Fire of love;
Hear us, HOLY SPIRIT.

Thou by Whom a Virgin bore
Him Whom Heaven and earth adore,
Sent our nature to restore;
Hear us, HOLY SPIRIT.

Thou Whom JESUS from His throne
Gave to cheer and help His own,
That they might not be alone;
Hear us, HOLY SPIRIT.

SPIRIT, guarding us from ill,
Bending right our stubborn will,
Though we grieve Thee, patient still;
Hear us, HOLY SPIRIT.

SPIRIT, strength of all the weak,
Giving courage to the meek,
Teaching faltering tongues to speak;
Hear us, HOLY SPIRIT.

SPIRIT, aiding all who yearn,
More of truth divine to learn,
And with deeper love to burn;
Hear us, HOLY SPIRIT.

SPIRIT, Whom by sin we grieve,
Whom the world will not receive,
Who dost help us to believe;
Hear us, HOLY SPIRIT.

Thou Who, when by sin we fall,
And when snares our souls enthral,
Lead'st us back with gentle call;
Hear us, HOLY SPIRIT.

That Thou wouldst Thy gifts bestow,
Gifts of wisdom GOD to know,
Gifts of strength to meet the foe,
Hear us, we beseech Thee

That to sin we may be dead,
And by Thee in meekness led
May the narrow pathway tread,
Hear us, we beseech Thee.

That whene'er we go astray,
Thine illuminating ray
Guide us to the truer way,
Hear us, we beseech Thee.

That we alway live to Thee
In all grace and purity,
Thine, for ever Thine, to be,
Hear us, we beseech Thee.

That all-holy as Thou art,
Thou wouldst dwell within our heart,
Never from us to depart,
Hear us, we beseech Thee.

Priest
LORD, have mercy.
Choir
LORD, have mercy.
Priest
CHRIST, have mercy.
Choir
CHRIST, have mercy.
Priest
LORD, have mercy.
Choir
rall.
LORD, have mer - cy.
Priest
Our FATHER.
Priest
℣ The SPIRIT of the LORD
Choir
℟ Fill - eth the world.
Priest
Let us pray.
Choir
A - men.

GOD, Who (as at this time) didst teach the hearts of Thy faithful people, by the sending to them the light of Thy HOLY SPIRIT; grant us by the Same SPIRIT to have a right judgment in all things, and evermore to rejoice in His holy comfort; through the merits of CHRIST JESUS our SAVIOUR, Who liveth and reigneth with Thee, in the unity of the Same SPIRIT, One GOD, world without end.

Litany of our Lord Jesus Christ

Priest or Two Cantors
LORD, have mer - cy.
Choir
LORD, have mer - cy.
Priest
CHRIST, have mer - cy.
Choir
CHRIST, have mer - cy.
Priest
LORD, have mer - cy.
Choir
LORD, have mer - cy.
Verse—FIRST TUNE
Response

Verse—Second Tune

Response

GOD the Father, God the Son,
Holy Ghost the Comforter,
Ever Blessed Three in One;
Hear us, Holy Trinity.

Word eternal, uncreate,
Maker of the universe,
God of God, and Light of Light;
Hear us, Holy Jesu.

I

WONDERFUL and Counsellor,
Father of eternity,
Mighty God, the Prince of peace;
Hear us, Holy Jesu.

Bruiser of the serpent's head,
Promised Seed of Abraham,
Judah's Lion, Israel's King;
Hear us, Holy Jesu.

Star of Jacob seen afar,
Healing Sun of righteousness,
Glorious Dayspring from on high;
Hear us, Holy Jesu.

Mighty Prophet, long foretold,
Fairest of the sons of men,
Captain of the hosts of God;
Hear us, Holy Jesu.

Stem of Jesse, righteous Branch,
David's Root and Offspring,
David's Son, and David's Lord;
Hear us, Holy Jesu.

Rose of Sharon, spotless Flower,
Lily of the valleys,
Vine of Israel, Tree of life;
Hear us, Holy Jesu.

Royal Babe of Bethlehem,
Word Incarnate, Virgin-born,
Son of Mary, Son of God;
Hear us, Holy Jesu.

Christ our Prophet, Priest, and King,
God with us, Emmanuel,
Very God and Very Man;
Hear us, Holy Jesu.

Hidden Manna, Bread of life
That cometh down from Heaven,
Wine that makest glad our hearts;
Hear us, Holy Jesu.

Light of Doctors, Martyrs' Strength,
Spouse of Virgins, Crown of Saints,
Joy of Angels, King of Heaven;
Hear us, Holy Jesu.

II

FROM the devil's wiles and snares,
From all fleshly passions,
From the world's deceitful pomp;
Save us, Holy Jesu.

From the poison-root of pride,
From all hate and jealousy,
From all sloth and deadly sin;
Save us, Holy Jesu.

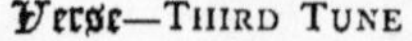
Verse—Third Tune

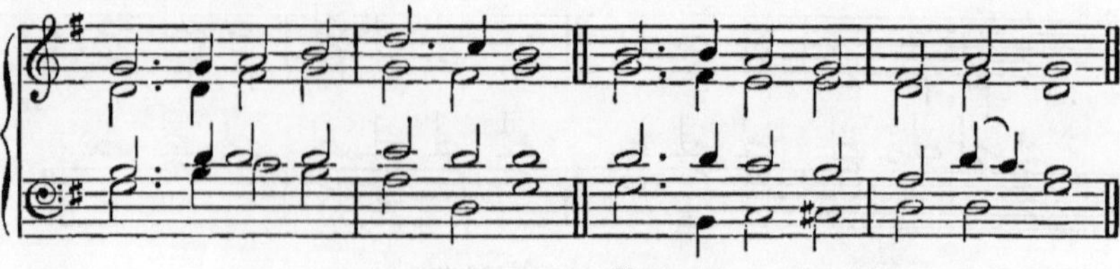

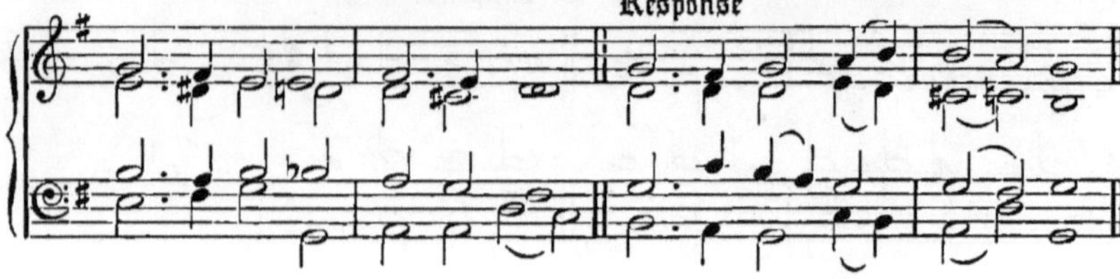
Response

III

BY the Spirit's quickening power
 Overshadowing Mary,
By Thy Birth as Man with men;
 Save us, Holy Jesu.

By the Shedding of Thy Blood,
On the eighth day circumcised,
When Thy sufferings first began;
 Save us, Holy Jesu.

By Thine Offering of Thyself
In Thy blessed Mother's arms,
To the Father consecrate;
 Save us, Holy Jesu.

By Thy gracious Love that called
Eastern Sages from afar,
With their gifts to worship Thee;
 Save us, Holy Jesu.

By Thy Journey long and drear,
Fleeing from King Herod's wrath,
Outcast exile from Thy home;
 Save us, Holy Jesu.

By the meek and humble Toil
In Thy work at Nazareth,
Subject to Thy parents' will;
 Save us, Holy Jesu.

IV

BY Thy Fast of forty days
 In the lonely wilderness,
When the tempter was o'erthrown;
 Save us, Holy Jesu.

By Thy Life of toil on earth
Full of love and mercy,
Tender Shepherd of the sheep;
 Save us, Holy Jesu.

By the yielding of Thy will,
By the precious Blood that flowed
In Thy sweat and agony;
 Save us, Holy Jesu.

By Thy Look on Peter turned,
In the dreadful judgment hall,
Look of pardon, look of love;
 Save us, Holy Jesu.

By the Scourging and the Shame,
By the Reed in mockery given,
By the Robe and Crown of thorn;
 Save us, Holy Jesu.

By Thy Death that conquered death,
By Thy Rising from the grave,
By Thy Going up on high;
 Save us, Holy Jesu.

When the Archangel's voice shall sound,
And the dead again shall rise,
In that awful Judgment Day;
 Good Lord, remember me.

Priest
LORD, have mer - cy.
Choir
LORD, have mer - cy.
Priest
CHRIST, have mer - cy.
Choir
CHRIST, have mer - cy.
Priest
LORD, have mer - cy.
Choir
LORD, have mer - cy.
Priest
Our FATHER.
Priest
℣ The WORD was made flesh, and dwelt a - mong us.
Choir
℟ And we be - held His glo - - ry.
Priest
Let us pray.
Choir
A - - men.

WE beseech Thee, O LORD, pour Thy grace into our hearts; that, as we have known the Incarnation of Thy SON JESUS CHRIST by the message of an Angel, so by His Cross and Passion we may be brought unto the glory of His Resurrection; through the Same JESUS CHRIST our LORD.

Litany for Saints' Days

Choir
Priest or Two Cantors
LORD, have mer - cy.
LORD, have mer - cy.
Choir
Priest
CHRIST, have mer - cy.
CHRIST, have mer-cy.
Choir
Priest
LORD, have mer - cy.
LORD, have mer-cy.
Verse—FIRST TUNE
Response

FATHER, on Thy heavenly throne,
  SON of GOD, in flesh made known,
SPIRIT, breathing o'er Thine own;
Hear us, Holy TRINITY.

JESU, lifted up on high,
On the Cross in agony,
O'er the stars triumphantly;
Hear us, Holy JESU.

I

JESU, drawing all to Thee,
  Sharers of Thy woes to be,
  Perfect bliss in Heaven to see;
Hear us, Holy JESU.

Sun, Whose rays of light divine
Through the clouds about Thee shine,
Clouds Whose beauties all are Thine;
Hear us, Holy JESU.

Thou the Angels' King and LORD,
Life of Saints, by all adored,
JESUS CHRIST, Incarnate Word;
Hear us, Holy JESU.

That with them who fought the fight,
And have won the crown of light,
Thou Thy servants wouldst unite;
Hear us, Holy JESU.

Verse—SECOND TUNE

Response

II

WITH Thy Mother, set on high,
Blest through all eternity
For her sweet humility;
King of Saints, unite us.

With the hosts who do Thy will,
That in war with powers of ill
We Thy purpose may fulfil;
King of Saints, unite us.

With the Baptist, Who alone
Made Thy great salvation known,
In the wild to Israel shewn;
King of Saints, unite us.

With the Patriarchal line,
Saints who longed to see Thee shine
O'er the world with light divine;
King of Saints, unite us.

With the Prophets, who of old,
Through afflictions manifold,
To the world Thy message told;
King of Saints, unite us.

With the Twelve on thrones of light,
Who erewhile in earthly night
Bare the burden of the fight;
King of Saints, unite us.

With the great inspirèd Four,
In whose page of sacred lore
Lives the Incarnate evermore;
King of Saints, unite us.

With the Infants for Thee slain,
Who by one short moment's pain
Everlasting joy did gain;
King of Saints, unite us.

With the Martyrs who o'ercame,
In the might of Thy dear Name,
Axe and torture, cross and flame;
King of Saints, unite us.

With the Bishops of Thy choice
Who obeyed their Master's voice,
And in glory now rejoice;
King of Saints, unite us.

With Thine own Confessors tried,
Who by Thee with strength supplied
Persecution's rage defied;
King of Saints, unite us.

With the Doctors, helped by Thee
In confounding heresy,
That our faith may constant be;
King of Saints, unite us.

With the Priests and Deacons pure,
Who did to the end endure,
Resting on Thy promise sure;
King of Saints, unite us.

With the Virgins, bound to Thee
By obedience, poverty,
And devoted chastity;
King of Saints, unite us.

And with all the unnumbered throng
Who through ages all along
Sing the everlasting song;
King of Saints, unite us.

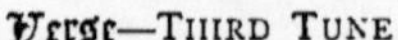
Verse—Third Tune

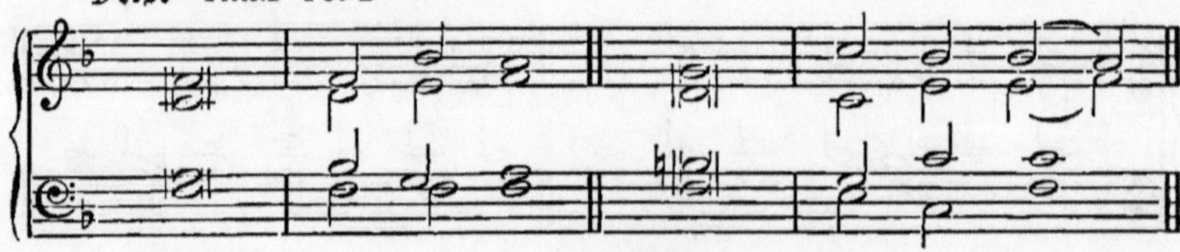

Response

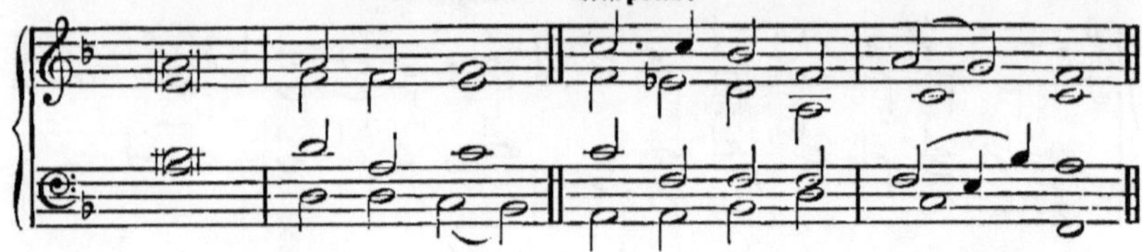

III

With the Simple | ones that heard,
And received Thy | Holy Word,
O'er the wise by | Thee preferred;
King of Saints, unite us.

With the Poor, to | Thee most dear,
Who though trouble | smote them here,
Heirs of Heaven | now appear;
King of Saints, unite us.

With the Mourners, | who below
Taught good seed in | tears to sow,
Now the fruit of | comfort know;
King of Saints, unite us.

With the Meek, whose | hidden worth,
In the day of | the new birth,
Shall inherit | all the earth;
King of Saints, unite us.

With the Souls, who | in distress
Thirsted for, and | now possess,
Thee, the Lord, their | Righteousness;
King of Saints, unite us.

With the Merci-| ful, who reign
Purified from | every stain,
Where Thy mercy | they obtain;
King of Saints, unite us.

With the Pure in | heart, whose sight,
Turned away from | vain delight,
Shall behold the | Infinite;
King of Saints, unite us.

With Thy Children, | who for Peace
Ever strove and | would not cease,
Till from strife they | found release;
King of Saints, unite us.

With the Just, whose | faith and love
Persecution | could not move,
In the joy of | Heaven above,
King of Saints, unite us.

IV

That, in one com-| munion blest,
We that war and | they that rest
May be as Thine | own confest,
Hear us, we beseech Thee.

That their followers | we may be,
Who themselves have | followed Thee,
Till with them Thy | face we see,
Hear us, we beseech Thee.

That where'er Thy | goings tend,
We our wayward | steps may bend
Till we reach Thee | in the end,
Hear us, we beseech Thee.

From the grave that | we may rise,
Hailing through the | opening skies
Thee our ever-| lasting Prize,
Hear us, we beseech Thee.

Priest
LORD, have mer - cy.
Choir
LORD, have mer - cy.
Priest
CHRIST, have mer - cy.
Choir
CHRIST, have mer - cy.
Priest
LORD, have mer - cy.
Choir
LORD, have mer - cy.
Priest
Our FATHER.
Priest
℣ Who are these that fly as a cloud,
Choir
℟ And as the doves to their win - dows?
Priest
Let us pray.
Choir
A - men.

O ALMIGHTY GOD, Who hast knit together Thine elect in one communion and fellowship, in the mystical Body of Thy SON CHRIST our LORD; grant us grace so to follow Thy blessed Saints, in all virtuous and godly living, that we may come to those unspeakable joys, which Thou hast prepared for them that unfeignedly love Thee; through JESUS CHRIST our LORD.

Litany of the Holy Angels

Choir
Priest or Two Cantors
LORD, have mer - cy.
LORD have mer - cy.
Choir
Priest
CHRIST, have mer - cy.
CHRIST, have mer - cy.
Choir
rall.
Priest
LORD, have mer - cy.
LORD, have mer - cy.
—Verse—FIRST TUNE
Response

LORD, have mercy.
CHRIST, have mercy.
LORD, have mercy.

GOD the FATHER, GOD the SON,
GOD the SPIRIT, Three in One,
While eternal ages run;
Hear us, Holy TRINITY.

I

CHRIST, the Angels' LORD and King,
Whom their cohorts sweetly sing
Circling round in ninefold ring;
Praise to Thee, LORD JESU.

For Saint Michael, Prince of might,
Captain of the Sons of light,
Who the dragon put to flight;
Praise to Thee, LORD JESU.

For the words that sweetly fell
On her heart who stored them well,
From the lips of Gabriel;
Praise to Thee, LORD JESU.

For Saint Raphael, healer, guide,
Constant by the traveller's side,
Guard on land and ocean's tide;
Praise to Thee, LORD JESU.

For the holy Cherubim,
For the shining Seraphim,
Lifting up their threefold hymn;
Praise to Thee, LORD JESU.

For the Guardian Angel dear
Thou dost send to guide and cheer,
Ever watchful, ever near;
Praise to Thee, LORD JESU.

For the constant love, which bears
All our wayward fears and cares,
Cheers our gloom, our sorrow shares;
Praise to Thee, LORD JESU.

II

THAT the Hosts who wait on Thee,
Who Thy love for mortals see,
May our loving Guardians be,
Hear us, we beseech Thee.

That their ceaseless homage paid
In the house no hands have made
May our feeble worship aid,
Hear us, we beseech Thee.

That they may, encamped around,
Watch, and keep the sacred ground,
Where Thy faithful ones are found,
Hear us, we beseech Thee.

That these glorious spirits bright
May o'ershadow us with light,
Whilst we daily wage the fight,
Hear us, we beseech Thee.

That their fearless, firm array
Guard for us the narrow way,
Watching while Thy people pray,
Hear us, we beseech Thee.

That their help may be at hand,
When amidst the flames we stand
By our sinful passions fanned,
Hear us, we beseech Thee.

That their sheltering wings protect
Every hour Thine own elect,
And their onward steps direct;
Hear us, we beseech Thee.

III

WHEN we faint, may they defend,
When we languish, may they tend,
Aid and cherish till the end;
Hear us, we beseech Thee.

When the dews of death fall fast,
Time of trial all but past,
May they bring us home at last;
Hear us, we beseech Thee.

May they then with holy care
Into Abraham's bosom bear
Those who Thine own Image wear;
Hear us, we beseech Thee.

May they from Thy holy hill,
Where they alway do Thy will,
Succour and defend us still;
Hear us, we beseech Thee.

That at last, the judgment o'er,
We may Thee, our LORD, adore,
With the Angels evermore,
Hear us, we beseech Thee.

Verse—SECOND TUNE

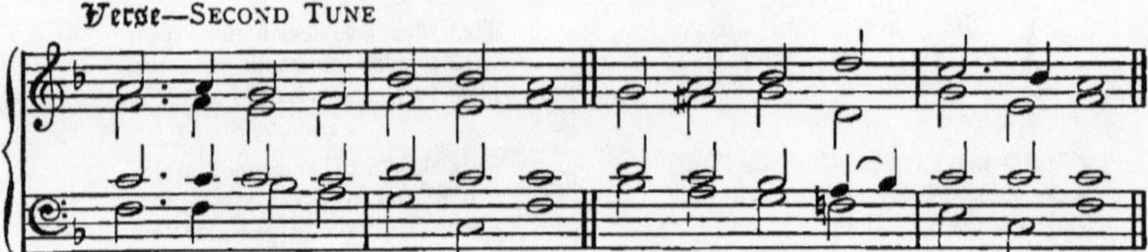

Response

II

THAT the Hosts who wait on Thee,
Who Thy love for mortals see,
May our loving Guardians be,
Hear us, we beseech Thee.

That their ceaseless homage paid
In the house no hands have made
May our feeble worship aid,
Hear us, we beseech Thee.

That they may, encamped around,
Watch, and keep the sacred ground,
Where Thy faithful ones are found,
Hear us, we beseech Thee.

That these glorious spirits bright
May o'ershadow us with light,
Whilst we daily wage the fight,
Hear us, we beseech Thee.

That their fearless, firm array
Guard for us the narrow way,
Watching while Thy people pray,
Hear us, we beseech Thee.

That their help may be at hand,
When amidst the flames we stand
By our sinful passions fanned,
Hear us, we beseech Thee.

That their sheltering wings protect
Every hour Thine own elect,
And their onward steps direct,
Hear us, we beseech Thee.

III

WHEN we faint, may they defend,
When we languish, may they tend,
Aid and cherish till the end;
Hear us, we beseech Thee.

When the dews of death fall fast,
Time of trial all but past,
May they bring us home at last;
Hear us, we beseech Thee.

May they then with holy care
Into Abraham's bosom bear
Those who Thine own Image wear;
Hear us, we beseech Thee.

May they from Thy holy hill,
Where they alway do Thy will,
Succour and defend us still;
Hear us, we beseech Thee.

That at last, the judgment o'er,
We may Thee, our LORD, adore,
With the Angels evermore,
Hear us, we beseech Thee.

Choir
Priest
LORD, have mer - cy.
LORD, have mer - cy.
Choir
Priest
CHRIST, have mer - cy.
CHRIST, have mer - cy.
Choir
rall.
Priest
LORD, have mer - cy.
LORD, have mer - cy.
Priest
Our FATHER.
Priest
℣ He shall give His Angels charge over thee,
Choir
℟ To keep thee . . in all thy ways.
Priest
Let us pray.
Choir
A - men.

O EVERLASTING GOD, Who hast ordained and constituted the services of Angels and men in a wonderful order; mercifully grant, that as Thy holy Angels alway do Thee service in Heaven, so by Thy appointment they may succour and defend us on earth; through JESUS CHRIST our LORD.

Litany for the Church

Priest or Two Cantors
LORD, have mer - cy.
Choir
LORD, have mer - cy.
Priest
CHRIST, have mer - cy.
Choir
CHRIST, have mer - cy.
Priest
LORD, have mer - cy.
Choir
LORD, have mer - cy.
Verse—FIRST TUNE
Response

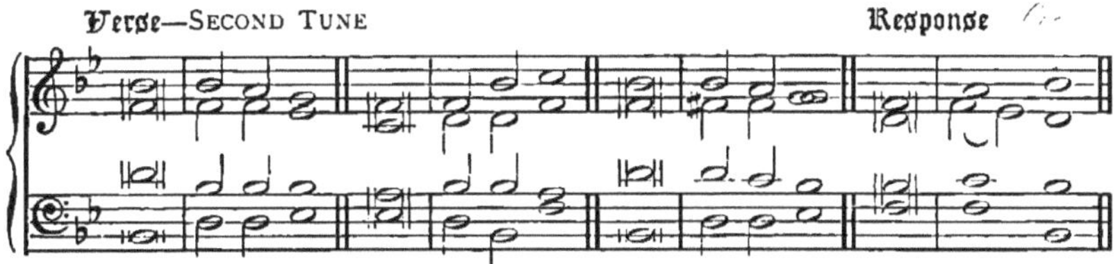
Verse—Second Tune
Response

FATHER, Lord of | Heaven above,
Son of God, In- | carnate Love,
Holy Spirit, | mystic Dove;
Hear us, Holy | Trinity.

Thou the Ever- | lasting Word,
In the highest | Heaven adored,
Thou the King, and | Thou the Lord;
Hear us, Holy | Jesu.

Who from out Thy | pierced side,
By the stream of | double tide,
Form'dst the Church, Thy | chosen Bride;
Hear us, Holy | Jesu.

I

THOU from Whom, their | living Head,
All Thy members | still are fed,
Knit together, | perfected;
Hear us, Holy | Jesu.

Throned at God the | Father's side,
Shedding forth up- | on Thy Bride
Thine own Spirit | for her Guide;
Hear us, Holy | Jesu.

Jesu, by Whose | master-hand
Firmly built Thy | Church doth stand,
Preaching truth in | every land;
Hear us, Holy | Jesu.

Thou Who dost Thy | Church defend,
And Thy promised | succour send,
Dwelling with her | to the end;
Hear us, Holy | Jesu.

Thou Who at the | last Great Day
Wilt Thy holy | Bride display
Deck'd in pure and | white array;
Hear us, Holy | Jesu.

Great High Priest, Who | still dost plead,
Living aye to | intercede
For each daily | want and need;
Hear us, Holy | Jesu.

Who, though now we | sow in tears,
Yet wilt drive a- | way our fears,
When the sign in | Heaven appears;
Hear us, Holy | Jesu.

II

BY Thy Wounds and | thorn-crowned Head,
By Thy Blood for | sinners shed,
By Thy Rising | from the dead;
Save us, Holy | Jesu.

By Thy Mounting | up on high
To Thy throne a- | bove the sky,
There to reign e- | ternally;
Save us, Holy | Jesu.

By the Coming | of the Lord,
Holy Ghost by | all adored
In the tongues of | fire outpoured;
Save us, Holy | Jesu.

Verse—THIRD TUNE

Response

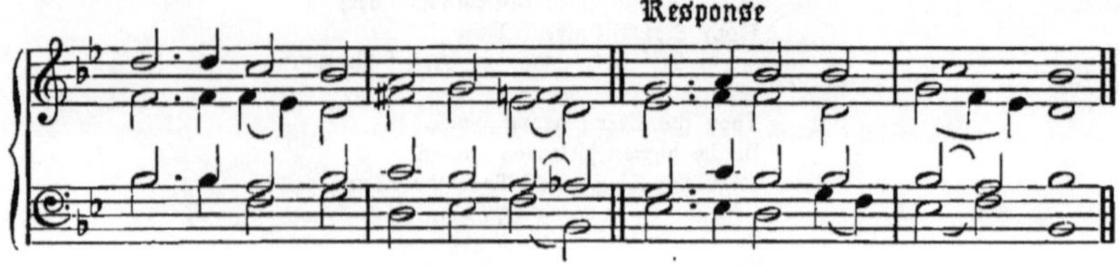

II

BY Thy Wounds and thorn-crowned Head,
By Thy Blood for sinners shed,
By Thy Rising from the dead;
Save us, Holy JESU.

By Thy Mounting up on high
To Thy throne above the sky,
There to reign eternally;
Save us, Holy JESU.

By the Coming of the LORD,
HOLY GHOST by all adored
In the tongues of fire outpoured;
Save us, Holy JESU.

III

THAT Thy flock, now gone astray
In the dark and stormy day,
May be led in Thy true way,
Hear us, we beseech Thee.

That to us Thou wouldst increase
Concord, unity, and peace,
Making all dissensions cease,
Hear us, we beseech Thee.

That Thou wouldst our missions bless,
Turning hearts to righteousness,
Till the world Thy Name confess,
Hear us, we beseech Thee.

That when fields to harvest white
Thy true labourers invite,
Thou wouldst send them in Thy might,
Hear us, we beseech Thee.

That Thy Priests in joy or ill,
Here may labour to fulfil
All Thy true and perfect will,
Hear us, we beseech Thee.

That Thou wouldst in them reveal
Courage, faithfulness, and zeal,
Power to warn, and grace to heal,
Hear us, we beseech Thee.

That Thou wouldst preserve them whole
Under Thy supreme control,
Safe in body and in soul,
Hear us, we beseech Thee.

That Thy Church may never yield
Faith in Thee, her constant Shield,
Till she win the well-fought field,
Hear us, we beseech Thee.

That, O Ruler of the fight,
Overcoming by Thy might
She may shine in heavenly light,
Hear us, we beseech Thee.

Priest
LORD, have mer - cy.
Choir
LORD, have mer - cy.
Priest
CHRIST, have mer - cy.
Choir
CHRIST, have mer - cy.
Priest
LORD, have mer - cy.
Choir
LORD, have mer - cy.
Priest
Our FATHER.
Priest
℣ Turn Thee again, Thou GOD of Hosts.
Choir
℟ Behold and vi - sit this . . Vine.
Priest
Let us pray.

LORD, we beseech Thee to keep Thy household the Church in continual godliness; that through Thy protection it may be free from all adversities, and devoutly given to serve Thee in good works, to the glory of Thy Name; through JESUS CHRIST our LORD.

Choir
A - men.

Litany of the Blessed Sacrament

Choir
Priest or Two Cantors
LORD, have mercy.
LORD, have mercy.
Choir
Choir
Priest
CHRIST, have mercy.
Priest
CHRIST, have mercy.
LORD, have mercy.
LORD, have mer - cy.
Verse
Response

GOD the FATHER, | GOD the Word,
GOD the HOLY | GHOST adored,
Blessed TRINITY, | One LORD;
Hear us, Holy TRINITY.

GOD for man In- | carnate made,
Price for our re- | demption paid,
Lamb upon the | Altar laid;
Hear us, Holy JESU.

Spotless Victim, | sinless Priest,
Thou the Giver, | Thou the Feast,
Shared by greatest | and by least:
Hear us, Holy JESU.

Verse—Parts I and IV

Response

I

TREE of Life in Paradise,
Dew of blessing from the skies,
Whence the living waters rise;
Hear us, Holy JESU.

Shadowed by the Offering
Which Melchizedec did bring,
Priest of GOD, and Salem's King;
Hear us, Holy JESU.

Rainbow, pledge of mercy given,
Manna that came down from heaven,
Rock for weary pilgrims riven;
Hear us, Holy JESU.

Pillar of the cloud and light,
Guide by day, and Guard by night,
Presence veiled from human sight;
Hear us, Holy JESU.

Shew-bread in the Temple spread,
Holy Offering, purest Bread,
Food on which Thy priests are fed;
Hear us, Holy JESU.

Ark of covenanted grace,
Glory of the holy Place,
Radiance from the FATHER's face;
Hear us, Holy JESU.

Cake that spreadst alarm among
All the Midianitish throng,
Bread that mak'st Elijah strong;
Hear us, Holy JESU.

Thou in sacred type the Meal
Sin's dread poison brought to heal,
Thou redemption's Pledge and Seal;
Hear us, Holy JESU.

Corn of Fatness, Heavenly Vine,
Very Man, and Word Divine;
Present under earthly sign;
Hear us, Holy JESU.

Paschal Lamb, on that last night
Offered in the newer rite,
As the law passed out of sight;
Hear us, Holy JESU.

Thou Who life and comfort art,
Bread to stay the fainting heart,
Wine that dost true joy impart:
Hear us, Holy JESU.

Lamb Who once for all wast slain
Who didst bear the atoning pain,
And for evermore dost reign;
Hear us, Holy JESU.

Priest and Sacrifice for aye,
Purging all our sins away,
Pleading for us as we pray;
Hear us, Holy JESU.

IV

BE Thou with us in Thy might,
When before our dying sight
Worlds unknown come forth to light;
Hear us, we beseech Thee.

Feed us in that last dread hour,
Stay our weakness with Thy power,
Make the evil tempter cower;
Hear us, we beseech Thee.

Bid the mortal struggle cease,
Give our spirits safe release,
So shall we depart in peace;
Hear us, we beseech Thee.

Bid us welcome, gracious LORD,
To the joys which Thou hast stored
At the marriage supper board;
Hear us, we beseech Thee.

LAMB of GOD, we worship Thee,
Who from sin hast set us free;
Thine all praise and glory be;
Hear us, we beseech Thee.

Verse—Parts II and III

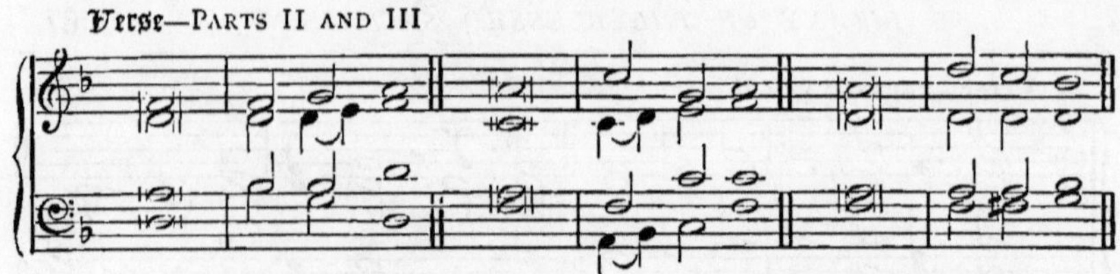

Response

II

From all unbe-| lief in Thee,
Who dost deign our | Food to be
In this wondrous | Mystery;
Save us, Holy Jesu.

From contempt and | proud offence,
Judging God by | human sense,
From all cold in-| difference;
Save us, Holy Jesu.

From a careless | drawing near,
Unrestrained by | love and fear,
To Thy Presence | veilëd here;
Save us, Holy Jesu.

From a heart which, | fed by Thee,
Takes Thy Gift un-| heedingly,
Leaves Thy Board un-| thankfully;
Save us, Holy Jesu.

III

By the love Thy | Cross displayed,
By the price Thy | Blood has paid,
By Thy full A-| tonement made;
Save us, Holy Jesu.

By Thy pleading | on the Throne
Thy One Offering | for Thine own,
On the heavenly | Altar shewn;
Save us, Holy Jesu.

By the Holy | Sacrifice
Offered here in | earthly guise,
One with That a-| bove the skies;
Save us, Holy Jesu.

That though here Thou | art unseen,
We by faith may | pierce the screen
Of the veils that | come between,
Hear us, we beseech Thee.

That Thou wouldst sup-| ply our need,
When with Prayer and | Praise and Creed
Thy great Sacri-| fice we plead,
Hear us, we beseech Thee.

That partaking, | we may be,
Soul and body, | kept by Thee
Unto life e-| ternally,
Hear us, we beseech Thee

Priest
Lord, have mercy.
Choir
Lord, have mercy.
Priest
Christ, have mercy.
Choir
Christ, have mercy.
Priest
Lord, have mercy.
Choir
Lord, have mer - - cy.
Priest
Our Father.
Priest
℣ Thou feddest Thine own people with An - gels' food.
Choir
℟ And didst send . . . them Bread . . . from Heaven.
Priest
Let us pray.
Choir
A - men.

O GOD, Who hast prepared for them that love Thee such good things as pass man's understanding; pour into our hearts such love toward Thee, that we, loving Thee above all things, may obtain Thy promises, which exceed all that we can desire; through Jesus Christ our Lord.

Litany of the Holy Childhood

Choir
Priest or Two Cantors
Lord, have mercy.
Lord, have mer - cy.
Choir
Priest
Christ, have mer - cy.
Christ, have mer - cy.
Choir
Priest
Lord, have mer - cy.
Lord, have mer - cy.
— Verse—First Tune
Response

LORD, have mercy.
CHRIST, have mercy.
LORD, have mercy.

GOD the FATHER, GOD the WORD,
GOD the HOLY GHOST adored,
Blessed TRINITY, One LORD;
Hear us, Holy TRINITY.

JESU, David's Root and Stem,
King of New Jerusalem,
Babe in lowly Bethlehem;
Hear us, Holy JESU.

I

JESU, SAVIOUR Meek and Mild,
Born for us a little Child,
Of the Virgin undefiled;
Hear us, Holy JESU.

JESU, by the Mother Maid
In Thy swaddling clothes arrayed;
In a lowly manger laid;
Hear us, Holy JESU.

JESU, at Whose infant feet,
Bending low in worship meet,
Shepherds knelt their LORD to greet;
Hear us, Holy JESU.

JESU, to Thy Temple brought,
Whom, by Thy Blest SPIRIT taught,
Simeon and Anna sought;
Hear us, Holy JESU.

JESU, unto Whom of yore
Wise Men, hasting to adore,
Gold and myrrh and incense bore;
Hear us, Holy JESU.

JESU, Who didst deign to flee
In Thy earliest infancy
Herod's ruthless cruelty;
Hear us, Holy JESU.

JESU, Whom Thy Mother found
Seated in the Temple's bound,
Midst the doctors gathered round;
Hear us, Holy JESU.

JESU, Name of highest worth,
Who to her who gave Thee birth
Wast obedient here on earth;
Hear us, Holy JESU.

II

FROM all pride and vain conceit,
Malice and unchastened heat,
From all lying and deceit;
Save us, Holy JESU.

From all sloth and idleness,
From indifference to distress,
From jealousy and greediness;
Save us, Holy JESU.

From ungrateful murmuring,
Thoughts in prayer time wandering,
From each sinful word and thing;
Save us, Holy JESU.

From all words and deeds of shame,
From dishonouring Thy Name
In the bodies Thou dost claim;
Save us, Holy JESU.

By Thy Coming from the skies,
By Thy Life in mortal guise,
Our Example and our Prize;
Save us, Holy JESU.

By Thy Birth and early Years,
By Thine infant Wants and Fears,
By Thy Sorrows and Thy Tears;
Save us, Holy JESU.

By Thy Wounds and thorn-crowned Head,
By Thy Blood for sinners shed,
By Thy Rising from the dead;
Save us, Holy JESU.

By Thine ever-conquering Might,
By Thy never-fading Light;
By Thy Mercies infinite;
Save us, Holy JESU.

Verse—Second Tune

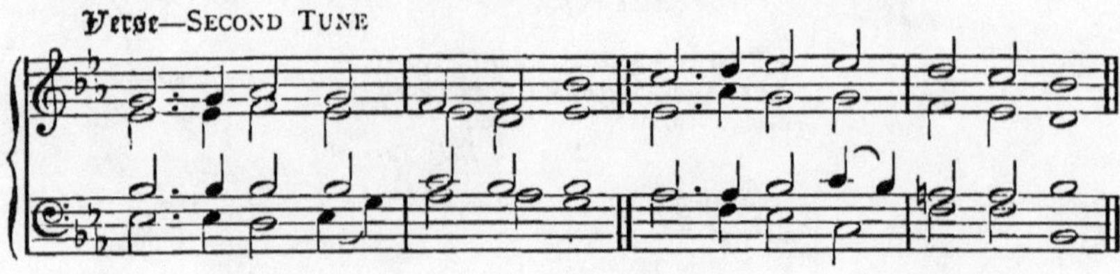

Response

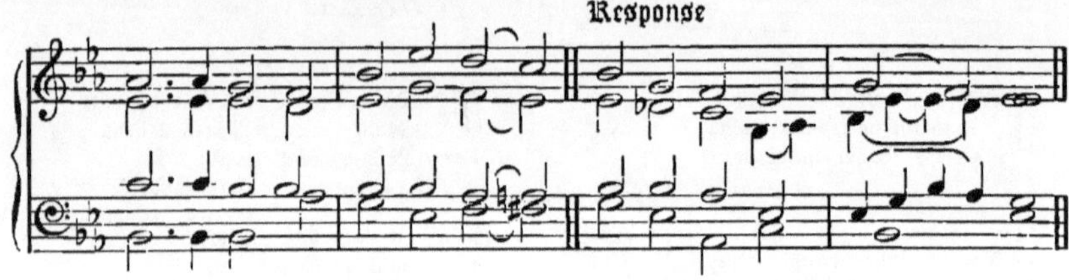

II

FROM all pride and vain conceit,
 Malice and unchastened heat,
From all lying and deceit;
 Save us, Holy Jesu.

From all sloth and idleness,
From indifference to distress,
From jealousy and greediness;
 Save us, Holy Jesu.

From ungrateful murmuring,
Thoughts in prayer time wandering,
From each sinful word and thing;
 Save us, Holy Jesu.

From all words and deeds of shame,
From dishonouring Thy Name
In the bodies Thou dost claim;
 Save us, Holy Jesu.

By Thy Coming from the skies,
By Thy Life in mortal guise,
Our Example and our Prize;
 Save us, Holy Jesu.

By Thy Birth and early Years,
By Thine infant Wants and Fears,
By Thy Sorrows and Thy Tears;
 Save us, Holy Jesu.

By Thy Wounds and thorn-crowned Head.
By Thy Blood for sinners shed,
By Thy Rising from the dead;
 Save us, Holy Jesu.

By Thine ever-conquering Might,
By Thy never-fading Light,
By Thy Mercies infinite;
 Save us, Holy Jesu.

III

THAT, like Isaac, we may dare
 By Thine aid our cross to bear,
And Thine awful Passion share,
 Hear us, we beseech Thee.

That, like Joseph, we may be
Strong from snares of flesh to flee,
Through the grace of chastity,
 Hear us, we beseech Thee.

That as Samuel heard Thy voice,
So may we, with ready choice,
At Thy gracious call rejoice,
 Hear us, we beseech Thee.

That as David did not fear
Bear or lion, sword or spear,
Strong in faith we may appear,
 Hear us, we beseech Thee.

That we may not be afraid
To make known Thy mighty aid,
Like the little captive maid,
 Hear us, we beseech Thee.

That like Daniel we endure,
Resting on Thy promise sure,
Midst the world's temptations pure,
 Hear us, we beseech Thee.

Most of all, that following Thee
Through Thy thirty years and three
Thy dear children we may be,
 Hear us, we beseech Thee.

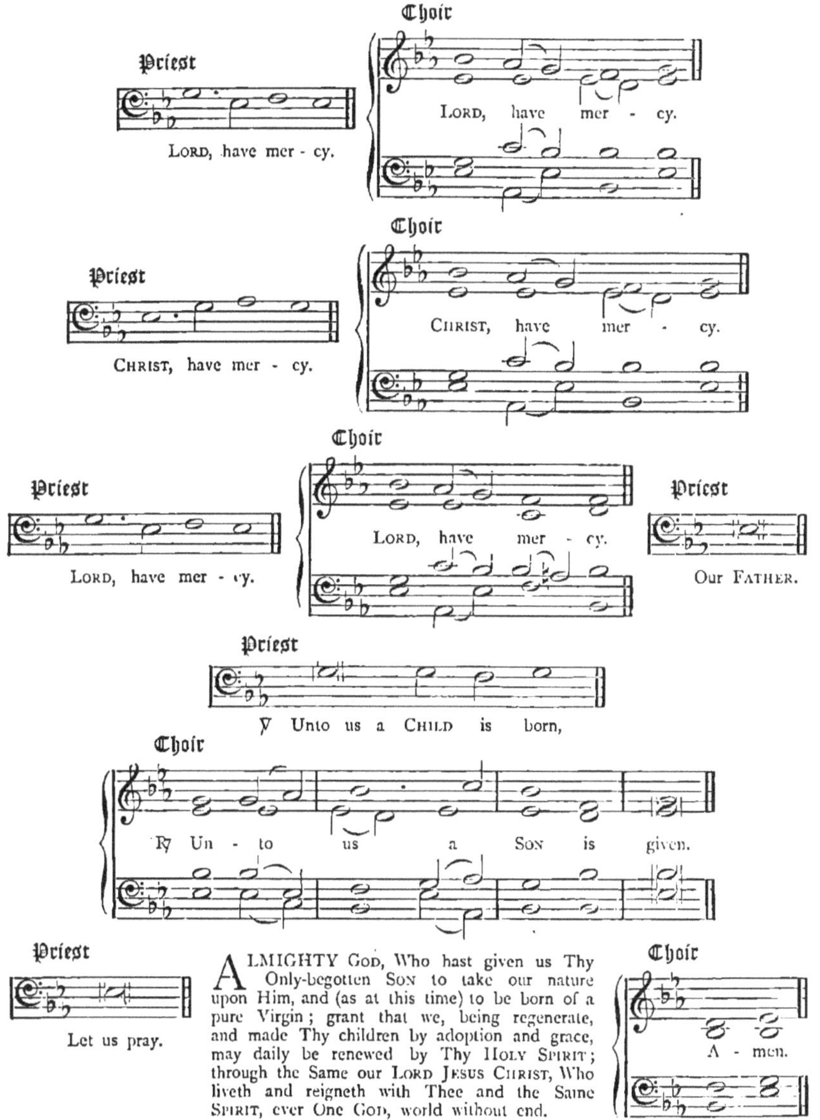

Priest
Lord, have mer - cy.
Choir
Lord, have mer - cy.
Priest
Christ, have mer - cy.
Choir
Christ, have mer - cy.
Priest
Lord, have mer - cy.
Choir
Lord, have mer - cy.
Priest
Our Father.
Priest
℣ Unto us a Child is born,
Choir
℟ Un - to us a Son is given.
Priest
Let us pray.
Choir
A - men.

Almighty God, Who hast given us Thy Only-begotten Son to take our nature upon Him, and (as at this time) to be born of a pure Virgin; grant that we, being regenerate, and made Thy children by adoption and grace, may daily be renewed by Thy Holy Spirit; through the Same our Lord Jesus Christ, Who liveth and reigneth with Thee and the Same Spirit, ever One God, world without end.

Litany in any Calamity

Choir
Priest or Two Cantors
LORD, have mercy.
LORD, have mer - cy.
Choir
Priest
CHRIST, have mer - cy.
CHRIST, have mercy.
Choir
Priest
LORD, have mer - cy.
LORD, have mercy.
Verse—FIRST TUNE
Response
dim.
p

LORD, have mercy.
CHRIST, have mercy.
LORD, have mercy.

O GOD the FATHER, grant us | peace in all our woe;
O GOD the SON, Thy grace and | mercy may we know;
O GOD the HOLY GHOST, Thy | inward light bestow;
Because against Thee have we sinned.

Prostrate, O HOLY LORD, all | we Thy servants lie,
And spread forth every secret | guilt before Thine eye;
To Thee, O GOD, for pardon | earnestly we cry;
Because against Thee have we sinned.

Receive the supplications | now before Thee poured,
And whatsoe'er we pray for | plenteously afford,
And upon all Thy people | shew Thy mercy, LORD;
Because against Thee have we sinned.

Thou meetest us with holy indig- | nation on our way,
For our sin's heavy load doth | grieve us day by day,
And without sign of light we | fail and faint away;
Because against Thee have we sinned.

For Thou dost know the woes that | hold our souls in thrall,
The evils all unnumbered | that on sinners fall;
And we invoke Thee, but Thou | hearest not our call;
Because against Thee have we sinned.

We lift our voices, for of | Thee we all have need,
And seeking Thee with peni- | tential tears we plead,
We have provoked Thine anger | by our own misdeed;
Because against Thee have we sinned.

Thee we implore; to Thee we | bring our mournful sighs;
Thy flock before Thee, JESU | CHRIST, all prostrate lies;
Now let Thy power bid us | from our woes arise;
Because against Thee have we sinned.

The meek confession of Thy | people's sin receive,
Which we pour forth before Thee, | while in tears we grieve,
While for our great transgression | heartfelt sighs we heave;
Because against Thee have we sinned.

* For peace we pray Thee; peace up- | on us all bestow;
Save us from battle | and from every woe,
LORD, we beseech Thee, all in | humble prayer laid low;
Because against Thee have we sinned.

Bow down Thine ear, O GOD, of | Thy great clemency;
Be every guilty sin-stain | washed away by Thee,
And from our perils of Thy | goodness set us free.
Because against Thee have we sinned.

* This stanza is only to be used in time of war.

Verse—Second Tune

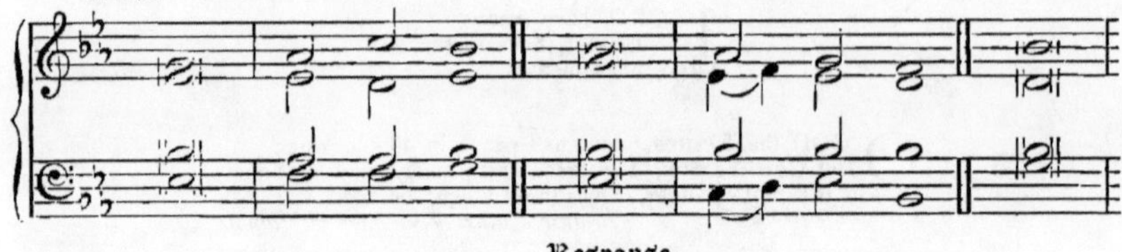

Response

O GOD the Father, grant us peace in | all our woe;
O God the Son, Thy grace and mercy | may we know;
O God the Holy Ghost, Thy | inward light bestow;
Because against Thee have we sinned.

Prostrate, O Holy Lord, all we Thy | servants lie,
And spread forth every secret guilt be- | fore Thine eye;
To Thee, O God, for pardon | earnestly we cry;
Because against Thee have we sinned.

Receive the supplications now be- | fore Thee poured,
And whatsoe'er we pray for plenteous- | ly afford,
And upon all Thy people | shew Thy mercy, Lord;
Because against Thee have we sinned.

Thou meetest us with holy indignation | on our way,
For our sin's heavy load doth grieve us | day by day,
And without sign of light we | fail and faint away;
Because against Thee have we sinned.

For Thou dost know the woes that hold our | souls in thrall,
The evils all unnumbered that on | sinners fall;
And we invoke Thee, but Thou | hearest not our call;
Because against Thee have we sinned.

We lift our voices, for of Thee we | all have need;
And seeking Thee with penitential | tears we plead,
We have provoked Thine anger | by our own misdeed;
Because against Thee have we sinned.

Thee we implore; to Thee we bring our | mournful sighs;
Thy flock before Thee, Jesu Christ, all | prostrate lies;
Now let Thy power bid us | from our woes arise;
Because against Thee have we sinned.

The meek confession of Thy people's | sin receive,
Which we pour forth before Thee, while in | tears we grieve,
While for our great transgression | heartfelt sighs we heave;
Because against Thee have we sinned.

* For peace we pray Thee; peace upon us | all bestow;
Save us from battle and from | every woe,
Lord, we beseech Thee, all in | humble prayer laid low;
Because against Thee have we sinned.

Bow down Thine ear, O God, of Thy great | clemency;
Be every guilty sin-stain washed a- | way by Thee,
And from our perils of Thy | goodness set us free;
Because against Thee have we sinned.

* This stanza is only to be used in time of war.

Priest
LORD, have mercy.
Choir
LORD, have mer - cy.
Priest
CHRIST, have mercy.
Choir
CHRIST, have mer - cy.
Priest
LORD, have mercy.
Choir
LORD, have mer - cy.
Priest
Our FATHER.
Priest
℣ Turn us then, O GOD our SA - VIOUR,
Choir
℟ And let Thine an - ger cease from us.
Priest
Let us pray.
Choir
A - men.

GRANT, we beseech Thee, Almighty GOD, that we, who for our evil deeds do worthily deserve to be punished, by the comfort of Thy grace may mercifully be relieved; through our LORD and SAVIOUR JESUS CHRIST.

Litany for a Happy Death

Choir
Priest or Two Cantors
LORD, have mer - cy.
LORD, have mer - cy.
Choir
Priest
CHRIST, have mer - cy.
CHRIST, have mer - cy.
Choir
Priest
LORD, have mer - cy.
LORD, have mer - cy.
Verse—FIRST TUNE
Response

Verse—Second Tune

Response

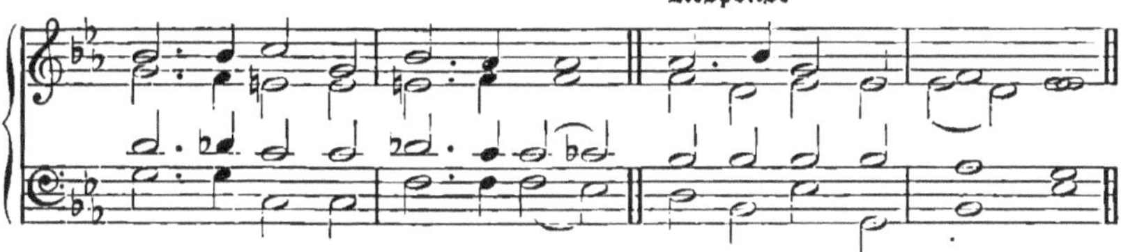

GOD the Father, God the Son,
With the Spirit ever One,
While eternal ages run;
Hear us, Holy Trinity.

Lord, to Whom Thy servants pray,
Creatures of a fleeting day,
Having here nor strength nor stay;
Hear us, Holy Jesu.

I

BY Whose grace, though sore distressed,
Tempted, troubled, and oppressed,
We may yet attain Thy rest;
Hear us, Holy Jesu.

Who in all our toil and woe
Strength and succour dost bestow,
Heavenly arms against the foe;
Hear us, Holy Jesu.

Who hast willed our life should be
Daily dying, Lord, with Thee,
Till by death Thou set us free;
Hear us, Holy Jesu.

Who one day wilt bring to view
All we think, or say, or do,
To be weighed in balance true;
Hear us, Holy Jesu.

Who unerringly dost know
When the soul for joy or woe
From its mortal home shall go;
Hear us, Holy Jesu.

Thou Who dost our nature wear,
Thou Who all our griefs didst share,
God of glory, Child of care;
Hear us, Holy Jesu.

Who that man with Thee may reign,
By the means Thou dost ordain
Bring'st Thy banished back again,
Hear us, Holy Jesu.

Who didst meekly bow Thy head
When Thy life-blood had been shed,
And wast numbered with the dead;
Hear us, Holy Jesu.

II

LOVE, Whom hate did crucify,
By Thy Going forth to die,
By Thy Lifting up on high;
Save us, Holy Jesu.

By Thy Body rent and torn,
By Thy Soul oppress'd with scorn,
By Thy Pains so meekly borne;
Save us, Holy Jesu.

By Thy Willingness to die,
By Thy loud and bitter Cry,
By Thy last expiring Sigh;
Save us, Holy Jesu.

Verse—Third Tune
Response

III

THAT through Thy most tender care
For Thy foes in Thy last prayer,
We in death no malice bear,
Hear us, we beseech Thee.

That as Thy benignity
Blessed the thief's repenting cry,
We shew mercy ere we die,
Hear us, we beseech Thee.

That on parent and on friend
We like Thee may forethought spend,
Still unselfish to the end,
Hear us, we beseech Thee.

That our earthly duties paid,
Pains of body may be stayed
By Thy thirsting unallayed,
Hear us, we beseech Thee.

That if desolation press,
We may think of Thy distress
In that awful loneliness,
Hear us, we beseech Thee.

That when body and when mind
Each hath suffered in its kind,
We may Thy perfection find,
Hear us, we beseech Thee.

That Thou wouldst our faith increase,
So our souls to glad release
We may yield in perfect peace,
Hear us, we beseech Thee.

IV

RISEN SAVIOUR, strong to save;
When beside the open grave
We Thy heavenly comfort crave,
Hear us, we beseech Thee.

Thou 'neath Whose protecting hand
Folded in the quiet land,
Rests in hope the chosen band,
Hear us, we beseech Thee.

Thou Who know'st what gifts of light
Bring them to the clearer sight
Of Thy glory infinite,
Hear us, we beseech Thee.

That Thy faithful ones may be
Blest and perfected in Thee,
Thine for all eternity;
Hear us, we beseech Thee.

V

THAT Thou wouldst Thine Angel send,
Constant guardian, faithful friend,
Us from Satan to defend,
Hear us, we beseech Thee.

That by penitence and prayer,
Daily searching, watchful care,
We our souls may now prepare,
Hear us, we beseech Thee.

That the absolving words be said,
That the holy Feast be spread,
Wine of Heaven, and living Bread,
Hear us, we beseech Thee.

That before our failing eyes,
Clearer visions may arise
Of the joys of Paradise,
Hear us, we beseech Thee.

That when ends this mortal strife,
Thou wouldst guide us, Light of life,
Through the land with shadows rife,
Hear us, we beseech Thee.

That our hand Thou wouldst hold fast,
And all toils and dangers past
Bring us to our home at last,
Hear us, we beseech Thee.

That Thou wouldst for ever be
Life to those who trust in Thee,
Life to all eternity,
Hear us we beseech Thee.

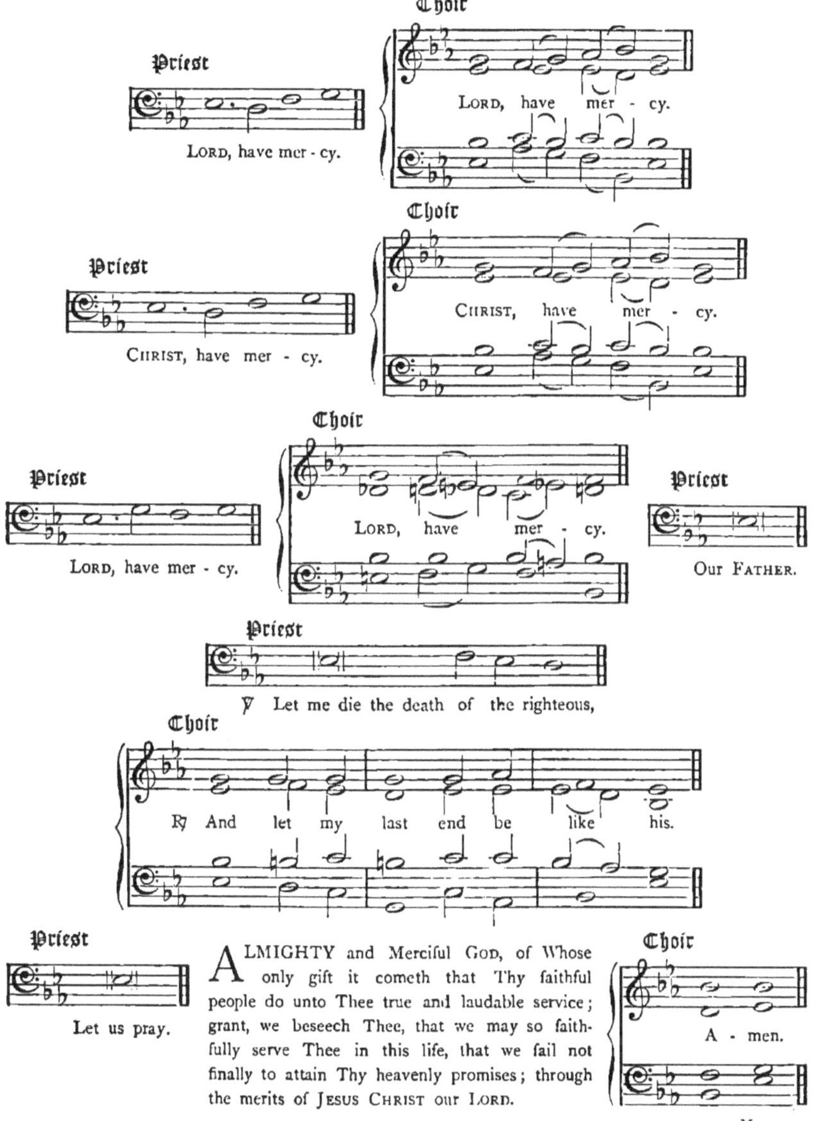
Priest
LORD, have mer - cy.
Choir
LORD, have mer - cy.
Priest
CHRIST, have mer - cy.
Choir
CHRIST, have mer - cy.
Priest
LORD, have mer - cy.
Choir
LORD, have mer - cy.
Priest
Our FATHER.
Priest
℣ Let me die the death of the righteous,
Choir
℟ And let my last end be like his.
Priest
Let us pray.
Choir
A - men.

ALMIGHTY and Merciful GOD, of Whose only gift it cometh that Thy faithful people do unto Thee true and laudable service; grant, we beseech Thee, that we may so faithfully serve Thee in this life, that we fail not finally to attain Thy heavenly promises; through the merits of JESUS CHRIST our LORD.

Advent

LITANY FOR ADVENT

Priest or Two Cantors
LORD, have mercy upon us
Choir
CHRIST, have mercy upon us.
Priest
LORD, have mercy upon us.
Priest
O CHRIST, hear us.
Choir
O CHRIST, gra - cious - ly hear us.
Priest
O GOD the FATHER, of Heaven,
Choir
Have mer - cy up - on us.

O GOD the SON, Re- | deemer of the | world,
O GOD the | HO-LY | GHOST,
HOLY | TRINITY, One | GOD,

O GOD, Who didst come to visit us in great hu- | mil-i- | ty,
Thou Who wilt come again with power | and great | glory,
Thou Who wilt | judge the | world,
Thou Who knowest the secrets | of all | hearts,

Have mercy upon us.

Thou Who wilt bring to light the hidden | things of | darkness,
Thou Who wilt make manifest the counsels | of the | heart,
Thou Who wilt bring every work | in-to | judgment,
Thou Who wilt separate the sheep | from the | goats,
Thou Who wilt set the sheep on Thy right hand, but the goats | on the | left,
Thou Who hast commanded all men everywhere | to re- | pent,

Have mercy upon us.

Priest
Be gracious to us,
Choir
And spare us, O LORD.
Priest
From all | e - vil.
Choir
Good LORD, de - li - ver us.
From all | sin,
From impenitence and | unbe-lief,
From neglect of Thy com- | mand-ments,
From forgetfulness | of Thee,
From | Thy wrath,
From a slumbering | con-science,
From an unpre- | pared death,
Good LORD, deliver us.
By Thy | great Com-passion,
By Thy | Long-suffering,
By Thy first Coming in | low-liness,
By Thy second Coming in | glo-ry,
In the | Hour of death,
In the | Day of judgment,
Good LORD, deliver us.
Priest
We | sin - ners,
Choir
We be - seech Thee to hear us, Good LORD.
That Thou wouldest vouchsafe to us | true re- | pentance,
That we may cast off the | works of | darkness,
That we may put on the | armour of | light,
That we may seek the LORD while He | may be | found,
That we may call upon Him while | He is | near,
That we may | watch and | pray,
That we may not be | found | sleeping,
That we may use aright the talent committed | to | us,
That we may be prepared to give an account of our | stew-ard- | ship
That we may find a merciful judgment at the | last | Day,
That we may attain to the resurrection | of the | just,
That we may receive a crown of | right-eous- | ness,
That we may enter into the joy of | our | LORD,
That Thou wouldest vouchsafe to all Thy faithful servants eternal | rest and | peace,
We beseech Thee to hear us, Good LORD.

Choir
Priest
We be-seech Thee to hear us.
Son of God,
Choir
Priest
. Spare us, O Lord.
O Lamb of God, That takest away the sins of the world,
Choir
Priest
Gra-cious-ly hear us, O Lord.
O Lamb of God, That takest away the sins of the world,
Choir
Priest
Have mer-cy up-on us.
O Lamb of God, That takest away the sins of the world,
Choir
Priest
O Christ, gra-cious-ly hear us.
O Christ, hear us.

Priest
LORD, have mercy upon us.
Choir
CHRIST, have mercy upon us.

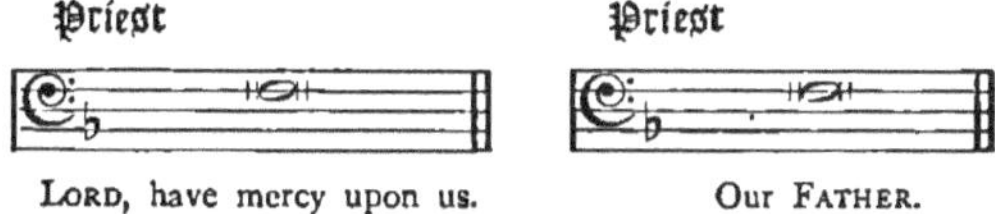
Priest
LORD, have mercy upon us.
Priest
Our FATHER.

Priest
℣ The LORD Whom ye seek shall suddenly come to His Tem - ple.

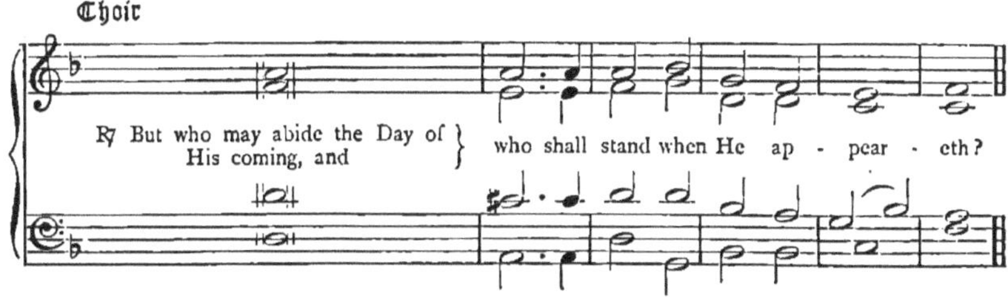
Choir
℟ But who may abide the Day of His coming, and
who shall stand when He ap - pear - eth?

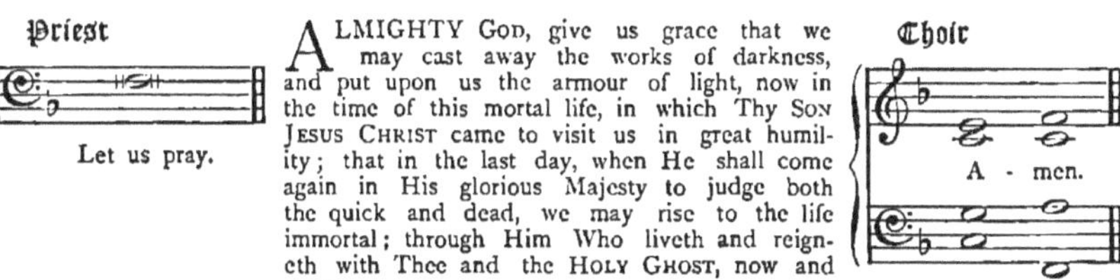
Priest
Let us pray.
Choir
A - men.

ALMIGHTY GOD, give us grace that we may cast away the works of darkness, and put upon us the armour of light, now in the time of this mortal life, in which Thy SON JESUS CHRIST came to visit us in great humility; that in the last day, when He shall come again in His glorious Majesty to judge both the quick and dead, we may rise to the life immortal; through Him Who liveth and reigneth with Thee and the HOLY GHOST, now and ever.

Lenten

LITANY

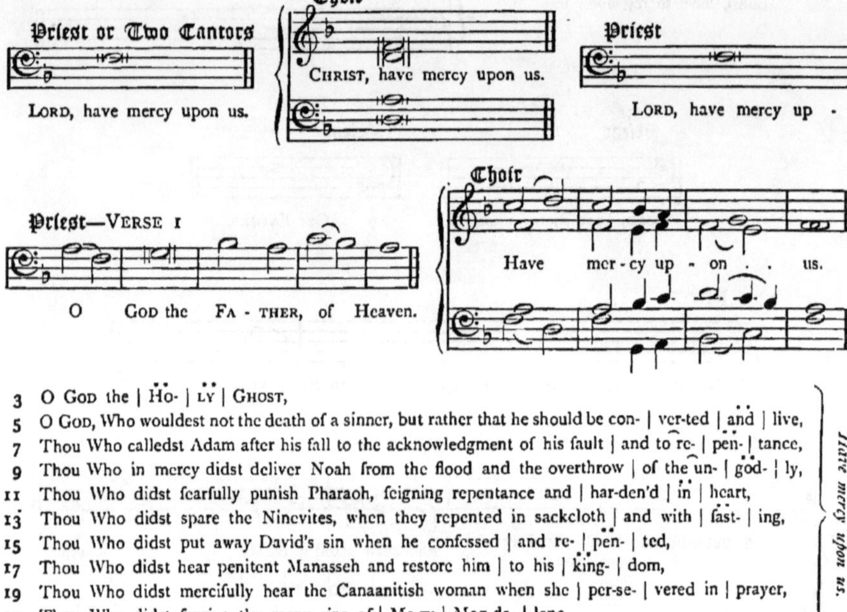

Priest or Two Cantors
LORD, have mercy upon us.
Choir
CHRIST, have mercy upon us.
Priest
LORD, have mercy up - -
Priest—VERSE I
O GOD the FA - THER, of Heaven.
Choir
Have mer - cy up - on . . us.

3 O GOD the | HO- | LY | GHOST,
5 O GOD, Who wouldest not the death of a sinner, but rather that he should be con- | ver-ted | and | live,
7 Thou Who calledst Adam after his fall to the acknowledgment of his fault | and to re- | pen- | tance,
9 Thou Who in mercy didst deliver Noah from the flood and the overthrow | of the un- | god- | ly,
11 Thou Who didst fearfully punish Pharaoh, feigning repentance and | har-den'd | in | heart,
13 Thou Who didst spare the Ninevites, when they repented in sackcloth | and with | fast- | ing,
15 Thou Who didst put away David's sin when he confessed | and re- | pen- | ted,
17 Thou Who didst hear penitent Manasseh and restore him | to his | king- | dom,
19 Thou Who didst mercifully hear the Canaanitish woman when she | per-se- | vered in | prayer,
21 Thou Who didst forgive the many sins of | Ma-ry | Mag-da- | lene,
23 Thou Who on the Cross didst promise Paradise | to the | peni-tent | thief,

Have mercy upon us.

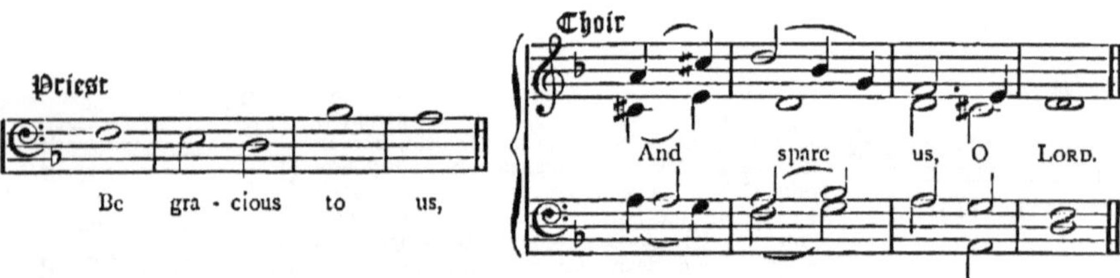

Priest
Be gra - cious to us,
Choir
And spare us, O LORD.

Season

OF PENITENCE

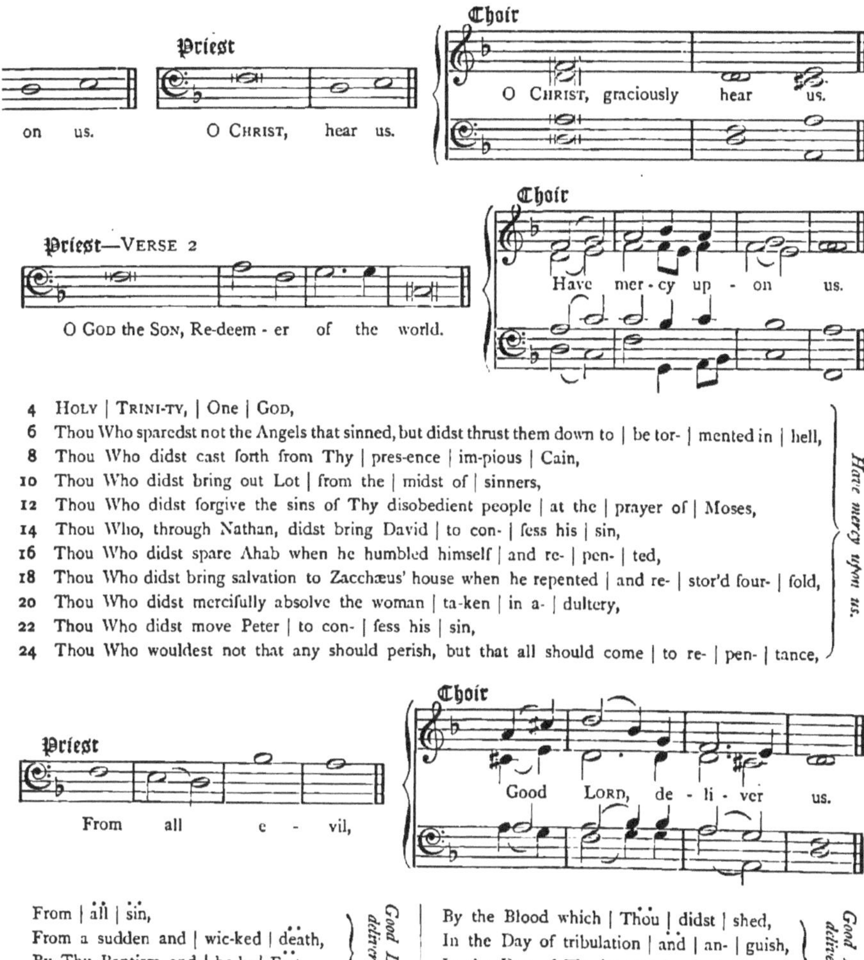
Priest
on us.
O Christ, hear us.
Choir
O Christ, graciously hear us.
Priest—Verse 2
O God the Son, Re-deem-er of the world.
Choir
Have mer-cy up-on us.
Priest
From all e-vil,
Choir
Good Lord, de-li-ver us.

4 Holy | Trini-ty, | One | God,
6 Thou Who sparedst not the Angels that sinned, but didst thrust them down to | be tor- | mented in | hell,
8 Thou Who didst cast forth from Thy | pres-ence | im-pious | Cain,
10 Thou Who didst bring out Lot | from the | midst of | sinners,
12 Thou Who didst forgive the sins of Thy disobedient people | at the | prayer of | Moses,
14 Thou Who, through Nathan, didst bring David | to con- | fess his | sin,
16 Thou Who didst spare Ahab when he humbled himself | and re- | pen- | ted,
18 Thou Who didst bring salvation to Zacchæus' house when he repented | and re- | stor'd four- | fold,
20 Thou Who didst mercifully absolve the woman | ta-ken | in a- | dultery,
22 Thou Who didst move Peter | to con- | fess his | sin,
24 Thou Who wouldest not that any should perish, but that all should come | to re- | pen- | tance,

Have mercy upon us.

From | all | sin,
From a sudden and | wic-ked | death,
By Thy Baptism and | ho-ly | Fast,
By Thy | Toils and | Griefs,

Good Lord, deliver us.

By the Blood which | Thou | didst | shed,
In the Day of tribulation | and | an- | guish,
In the Day of Thy | aw-ful | judg- | ment,

Good Lord, deliver us.

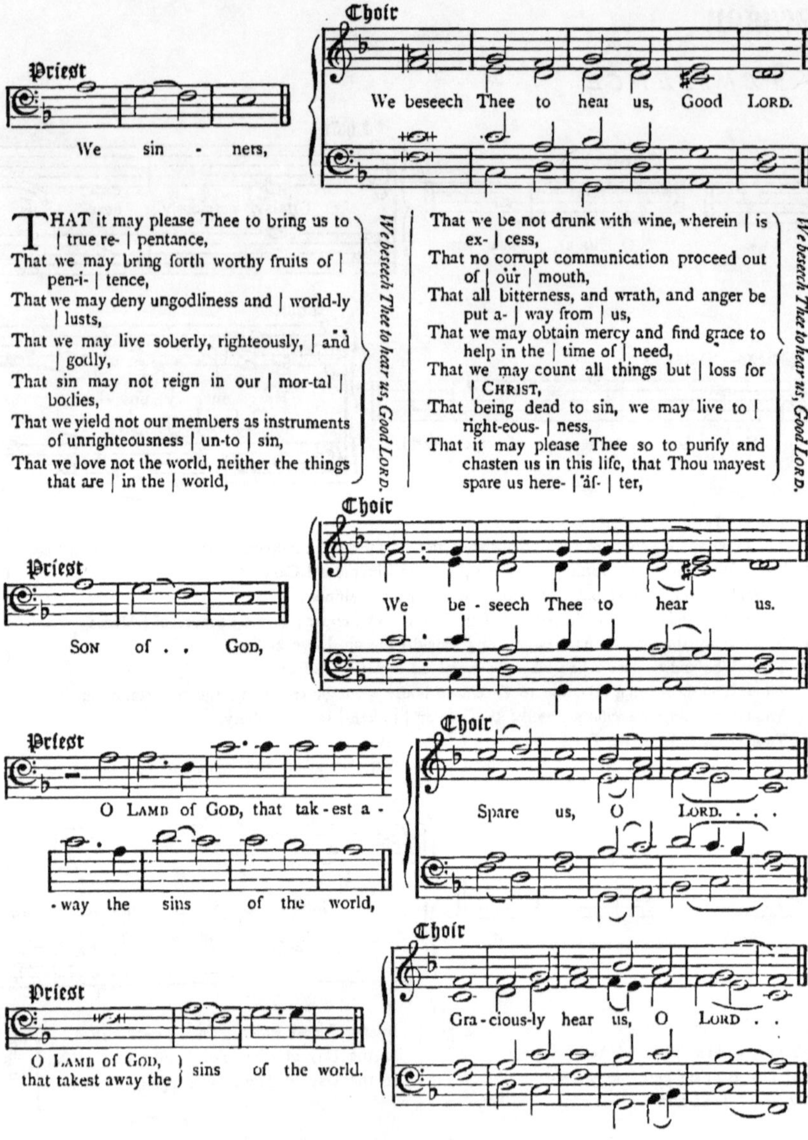
Priest
We sin - ners,
Choir
We beseech Thee to hear us, Good Lord.
That it may please Thee to bring us to | true re- | pentance,
That we may bring forth worthy fruits of | pen-i- | tence,
That we may deny ungodliness and | world-ly | lusts,
That we may live soberly, righteously, | and | godly,
That sin may not reign in our | mor-tal | bodies,
That we yield not our members as instruments of unrighteousness | un-to | sin,
That we love not the world, neither the things that are | in the | world,
We beseech Thee to hear us, Good Lord.
That we be not drunk with wine, wherein | is ex- | cess,
That no corrupt communication proceed out of | our | mouth,
That all bitterness, and wrath, and anger be put a- | way from | us,
That we may obtain mercy and find grace to help in the | time of | need,
That we may count all things but | loss for | Christ,
That being dead to sin, we may live to | right-eous- | ness,
That it may please Thee so to purify and chasten us in this life, that Thou mayest spare us here- | af- | ter,
We beseech Thee to hear us, Good Lord.
Priest
Son of . . God,
Choir
We be - seech Thee to hear us.
Priest
O Lamb of God, that tak - est a - - way the sins of the world,
Choir
Spare us, O Lord. . . .
Priest
O Lamb of God, that takest away the sins of the world.
Choir
Gra - cious-ly hear us, O Lord . .

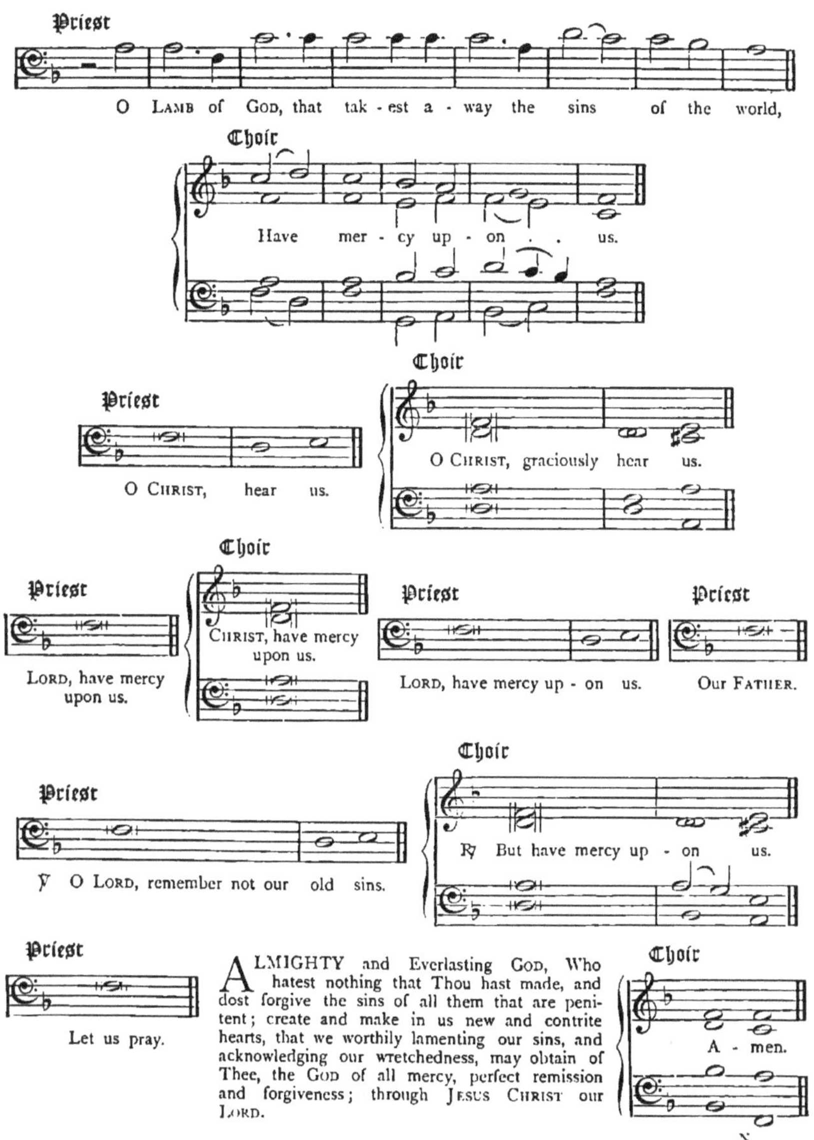
Priest
O Lamb of God, that tak - est a - way the sins of the world,
Choir
Have mer - cy up - on . . us.
Priest
O Christ, hear us.
Choir
O Christ, graciously hear us.
Priest
Lord, have mercy upon us.
Choir
Christ, have mercy upon us.
Priest
Lord, have mercy up - on us.
Priest
Our Father.
Priest
℣ O Lord, remember not our old sins.
Choir
℟ But have mercy up - on us.
Priest
Let us pray.
Choir
A - men.

ALMIGHTY and Everlasting God, Who hatest nothing that Thou hast made, and dost forgive the sins of all them that are penitent; create and make in us new and contrite hearts, that we worthily lamenting our sins, and acknowledging our wretchedness, may obtain of Thee, the God of all mercy, perfect remission and forgiveness; through Jesus Christ our Lord.

Litany of the Passion

Priest
LORD, have mer - cy up - on us.
Choir
CHRIST, have mer - cy up - on us.
Priest
LORD, have mer - cy up - on us.
Choir
Have mer - cy up - on us.
Priest
O GOD the FATHER, of Heaven.

O GOD the SON, Redeemer | of the world,
O GOD the | HO-LY GHOST,
HOLY TRINITY, | One GOD.

JESU, the eternal | Wis-dom,
JESU, meek King entering Je- | ru-sa-lem,
JESU, sold for thirty pieces of | sil-ver,
JESU, bent to wash Thy dis- | ci-ples' feet,
JESU, Who didst keep the Passover with Thy dis- | ci-ples,
JESU, Who gavest us Thy Body for food, Thy | Blood for drink,
JESU, in agony bathed in | blood-y sweat,
JESU, betrayed by Judas | with a kiss,
JESU, bound roughly by the | ser-vants,
JESU, forsaken by Thy dis- | ci-ples,
JESU, taken before Annas and | Cai-a-phas,
JESU, accused by false | wit-ness-es,
JESU, judged | worthy of death,
JESU, blindfolded, buffeted, and | spit up-on,
JESU, thrice denied by | Pe-ter,
JESU, delivered bound to | Pi-late,
JESU, mocked and set at nought by | He-rod,
JESU, clad in a | white robe,
JESU, rejected for Bar- | ab-bas,

Have mercy upon us.

JESU, cruelly cut with | scourg-ing,
JESU, clad in a purple robe, and | crowned with thorns,
JESU, mocked with a reed for a | scep-tre,
JESU, condemned to a | cru-el death,
JESU, laden with the | hea-vy Cross,
JESU, led as a sheep to the | slaugh-ter,
JESU, nailed | to the Cross,
JESU, crucified be- | tween two thieves,
JESU, blasphemed by the passers-by and derided | by the Jews,
JESU, mocked by the soldiers, and reviled by the | rob-ber,
JESU, presented with vinegar | in Thy thirst,
JESU, Who didst give up Thy Spirit to Thy | FA-THER,
JESU, pierced | by the lance,
JESU, from Whose side came | water and blood,
JESU, Who bare our sins in Thy Body | on the Tree,
JESU, taken down from the Cross, and laid in a new | se-pul-chre,
JESU, Who after death didst descend | in-to hell,
JESU, exalted | in-to Heaven,
JESU, our Advocate with the | FA-THER,

Have mercy upon us.

Priest
Be gracious to us.
Choir
And spare us, O Lord.
Priest
From all e - vil,
Choir
De - liv - er us, O Lord.

From a sudden and unpre- | pared death,
From the snares of the | de-vil,
From anger, hatred, and all | ill will,
From ever- | lasting death,
Deliver us, O Lord.

By Thine Agony and | bloody Sweat,
By Thy Cross and | Pass-ion,
By Thy Death and | Bu-rial,
By Thy holy Resur- | rec-tion,
In the Day of | judg-ment,
Deliver us, O Lord.

Priest
We sin - ners,
Choir
We be-seech Thee to hear us.

That being dead unto sin, we may live unto | right eous-ness,
That we glory not save in the Cross of our Lord | Je-sus Christ,
That we may crucify the flesh with its af- | fections and lusts,
That we may take up our cross daily and | fol-low Thee,
That what is gain to us we may count as | loss for Thee,
That we strive above all things to know Jesus | cru-ci-fied,
That Thy Blood may cleanse us from | all our sins,
That we may walk henceforth in | newness of life,
That we may follow the blessed steps of Thy most | ho-ly life,
That we may reign with Thee here- | af-ter,
We beseech Thee to hear us.

Choir
Priest
Son of God,
We be-seech Thee to hear us.
Priest
O Lamb of God, That tak - est a - way the sins of the world,
Org. Sw. Diaps.
Choir
p
Je - su, spare us.
Priest
O Lamb of God, That tak - est a - way the sins of the world,
[Accompaniment as before]
Choir
p
Je - su, hear us.

Priest
O LAMB of GOD, That tak - est a - way the sins of the world,
ORG. Sw. Diaps.
Choir
pp
dim.
JE - SU, have mer - cy up - on . . . us.
Priest
Our FATHER.
Priest
℣ O SAVIOUR of the world, Who by Thy Cross and precious Blood hast re - deem - ed us.
Choir mf cres - - cen - - do . . dim. rall. p
℟ Save us and help us, we hum - bly be - seech Thee, O LORD.
Priest
Let us pray.
Choir
A - men.

ALMIGHTY and Everlasting GOD, Who of Thy tender love towards mankind, hast sent Thy SON our SAVIOUR JESUS CHRIST, to take upon Him our flesh, and to suffer death upon the Cross, that all mankind should follow the example of His great humility; mercifully grant, that we may both follow the example of His patience, and also be made partakers of His resurrection; through the Same JESUS CHRIST our LORD.

Easter

LITANY OF THE

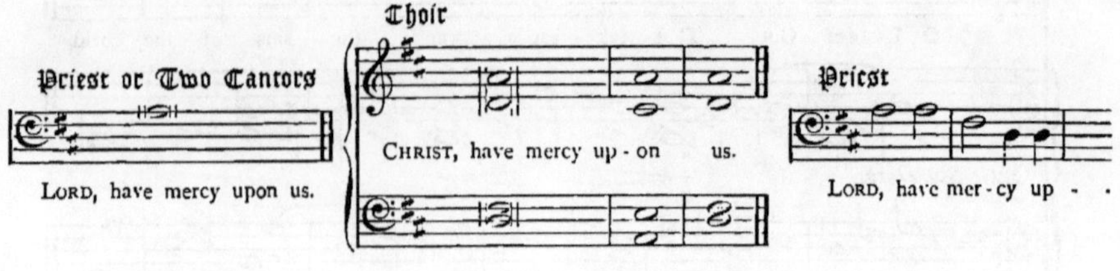
Choir
Priest or Two Cantors
LORD, have mercy upon us.
CHRIST, have mercy up - on us.
Priest
LORD, have mer - cy up - -

Choir
Priest—VERSE I
O GOD the FATHER, of Heaven.
Have mercy up - on us.

3 O GOD the | HO-LY | GHOST, the | Comforter,
5 JESU, our Paschal Lamb, Who wast offered for us, and hast taken away the | sins | of the | world,
7 JESU, Who by Thy Rising to life again hast restored to us | e-ver- | last-ing | life,
9 JESU, Who art Thyself the Resur- | rec-tion | and the | Life,
11 JESU, Who didst appear to | Ma-ry | Mag-da- | lene,
13 JESU, Who didst appear to the two disciples on the way to Emmaus, and wast known of them in the | Break-ing | of | bread,
15 JESU, Who didst confirm the faith of Thomas by shewing him Thy | hands | and Thy | feet,
17 JESU, Who didst commission | Peter to | feed Thy | sheep,
19 JESU, Who wast seen of above five hundred | breth-ren | at | once,

Have mercy upon us.

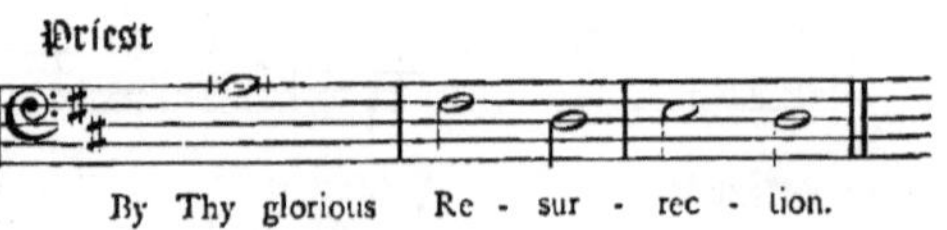
Priest
By Thy glorious Re - sur - rec - tion.

By Thy Victory | o-ver | death,
By the glorious Majesty of Thy | ri-sen | Bo-dy.

Tide

RESURRECTION

on us.

Priest

O CHRIST, hear us.

Choir

O CHRIST, gra-cious-ly hear us.

Priest—VERSE 2

O GOD the SON, REDEEMER of the world,

Choir

Have mer-cy up-on us.

4 HOLY TRINITY, | One | GOD,
6 JESU, Who by Thy Death hast de- | stroy-ed | death,
8 JESU, the Firstfruits of | them that | slept,
10 JESU, Who didst rise very early in the morning on the first day | of the | week,
12 JESU, Who didst send Thy angels to the women to say that | Thou wast | risen,
14 JESU, Who didst appear to the Eleven, and give | them Thy | peace,
16 JESU, Who didst shew Thyself to Thy disciples at the | Sea of | Tiberias,
18 JESU, Who didst converse with Thy disciples upon a mountain in | Gal-i- | lee,
20 JESU, Who livest and wast dead, and art alive for | e-ver- | more,

Have mercy upon us.

Choir
Good LORD, de - li - ver us.

Good LORD, deliver us.

Priest—Verse 1
We . . sin - ners,
Choir
We beseech Thee to hear us.
Priest—Verse 2
That as Thou wast raised up from the
3 That we may reckon ourselves to be dead indeed unto sin, but a- | live | un-to | God,
5 That we may | walk | in the | Spirit,
7 That we may walk in love as | Thou hast | lov-ed | us,
9 That we may set our affections on things above, not on | things | on the | earth,
11 That we may be- | hold Thy | face with | joy,
13 That we may | see Thee | as Thou | art,
15 That we may be made | e-qual | unto the | Angels,
We beseech Thee to hear us.
Choir—1st Response
Priest—Before each Response
O Lamb of God, That takest away the sins of the world.
Je - su,
Choir
Priest
O Christ, hear us.
O Christ, gra-cious-ly hear us.
Priest
Lord, have mercy
Choir
Priest
℣ When I awake up after Thy like - ness.
℟ I shall be sa - tis - fied with it.

Choir
dead by the glory of the FATHER, even so we also may walk in
new - ness of life,
We be - seech Thee to hear us.
Choir—2nd Response
spare us.
JE - SU, hear us.
Choir—3rd Response
JESU, have mer - cy up - on us.
Choir
upon us.
CHRIST, have mercy up - on us.
Priest
LORD, have mer-cy up - on us.
Priest
Our FATHER.

4 That we may not henceforth live unto ourselves, | but | un-to | Thee,
6 That we may crucify the flesh with its af- | fections | and | lusts,
8 That being risen with Thee, we may seek those things | which | are a- | bove,
10 That in the Last Day we may be set at | Thy | right | hand,
12 That we may be for ever with Thee | where | Thou | art,
14 That we may be made | like | un-to | Thee,
16 That we may dwell with Thee for | ever | in | Heaven,

We beseech Thee to hear us.

Priest

Let us pray.

ALMIGHTY GOD, Who through Thine Only-begotten SON JESUS CHRIST hast overcome death, and opened unto us the gate of everlasting life; we humbly beseech Thee, that, as by Thy special grace preventing us, Thou dost put into our minds good desires, so by Thy continual help we may bring the same to good effect; through JESUS CHRIST our LORD, Who liveth and reigneth with Thee and the HOLY GHOST, ever One GOD, world without end.

Choir

A - men.

Ascension

LITANY OF

Priest or Two Cantors

LORD, have mer-cy up-on us.

Choir

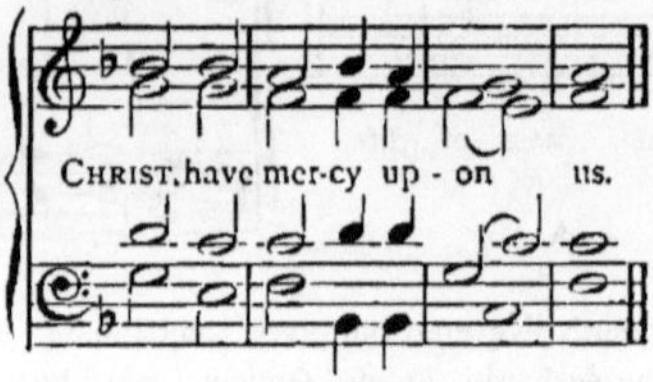

CHRIST, have mer-cy up-on us.

Priest

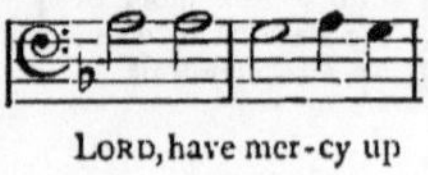

LORD, have mer-cy up

Priest—VERSE 1

O GOD the FATHER, of Heaven,

Choir

Have mer-cy up-on us.

3 O GOD the | HO-LY | GHOST,
5 JESU, King of | glo- | ry,
7 JESU, Who didst lead captivity captive, and gavest gifts | un-to | men,
9 JESU, seated in glory at the right Hand of the | FA- | THER,
11 JESU, crowned with glory and | ho- | nour,
13 JESU, of Whose kingdom there shall | be no | end,
15 JESU, Who art anointed with the oil of gladness a- | bove Thy | fellows,
17 JESU, Who hast opened the Kingdom of Heaven to | all be- | lievers,
19 JESU, Who hast entered into the Holy of | Ho- | lies,
21 JESU, Who didst send down Thy HOLY GHOST on | Thy dis- | ciples,
23 JESU, Who by the power of the HOLY GHOST art present with us in the Blessed | Sa-cra- | ment,
25 JESU, Who wilt come again in glory to | judge the | world,

Have mercy upon us.

Priest

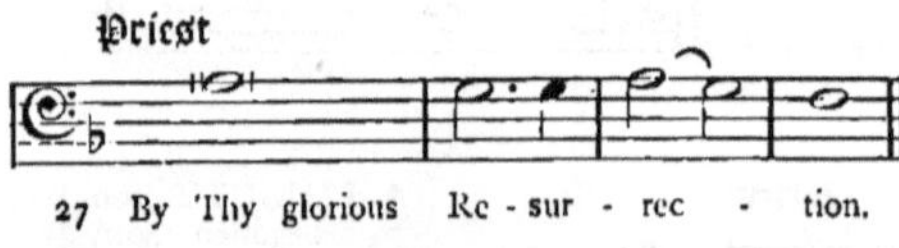

27 By Thy glorious Re-sur-rec-tion.

28 By Thy wondrous | As- | cen- | sion,
29 By Thine all-powerful | In-ter- | ces- | sion,
30 By Thy tri- | um-phant | Ma-jes- | ty,
31 By Thy Al- | migh-ty | Pow- | er,

Tide

THE ASCENSION

on us.
Priest
O Christ, hear us.
Choir
O Christ, gra-cious-ly hear us.
Priest—Verse 2
O God the Son, Re-deem-er of the world.
Choir
Have mer-cy up-on us.
Choir
Good Lord, de-liv-er us.

4 Holy | Trinity, | One | God,
6 Jesu, Who art | gone up | in-to | Heaven,
8 Jesu, at Whose Name | e-very | knee must | bow,
10 Jesu, unto Whom all power in Heaven | and in | earth is | given,
12 Jesu, Who must reign until Thou hast put all enemies | un-der | Thy | feet,
14 Jesu, adored by the | ho-ly | An- | gels,
16 Jesu, Who art the happiness of the Blessed, and | in Whose | presence is | life,
18 Jesu, our High Priest | for- | e- | ver,
20 Jesu, Who ever livest to make | in-ter- | ces-sion | for us,
22 Jesu, Who dost promise that whatsoever we ask in | Thy Name | Thou wilt | do it,
24 Jesu, Who art gone to prepare a | place | for | us,
25 Jesu, Who wilt receive Thine own unto Thyself, that they may be | with Thee | where Thou | art,

Have mercy upon us.

Good Lord, deliver us. .

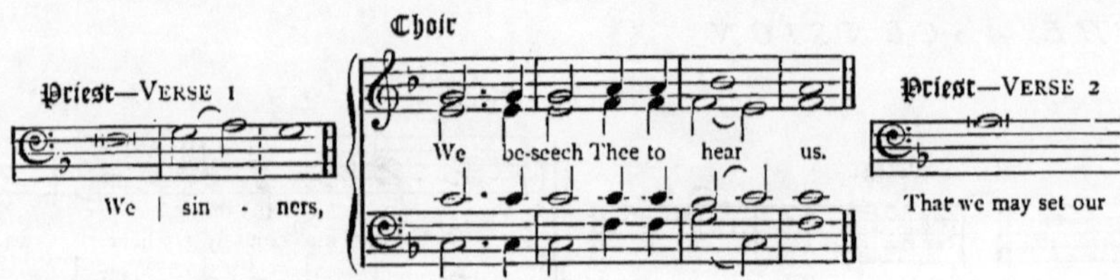
Choir
Priest—VERSE 1
We | sin - ners,
We be-seech Thee to hear us.
Priest—VERSE 2
That we may set our

3 That we may be holy and without blame before | Thee in | love,
5 That keeping Thy commandments, we may abide in | Thy | love,
7 That in Thee we | may have | peace,
9 That Thou wouldest pour down Thy HOLY SPIRIT up- | on the | Church,
11 That Thou wouldest give them the graces of courage, faithfulness, and | fer-vent | zeal,
13 That Thou wouldest preserve Thy Church from | all her | enemies,

We beseech Thee to hear us.

Choir—*1st Response*

Priest—*Before each Response*

O LAMB of GOD, That takest away the sins of the world.

Spare

Choir

Priest

O CHRIST, hear us.

O CHRIST, gra-cious-ly hear us.

Priest

LORD, have mer-cy up -

Choir

Priest

℣ GOD is gone up with a mer - ry noise,

℟ And the LORD with the sound of the trump.

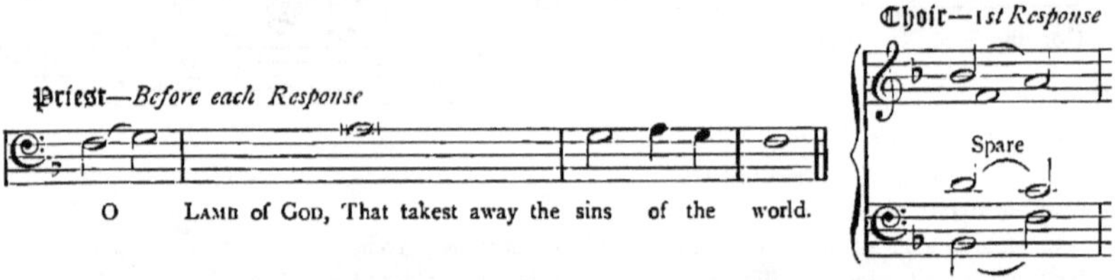

affections on things above, and not on things on the earth,
Choir
We be-seech Thee to hear us.
us, O Lord.
Choir—2nd Response
Hear us, O Lord.
Choir—3rd Response
Have mer-cy up-on us.
-on us.
Choir
Christ, have mer-cy up-on us.
Priest
Lord, have mer-cy up-on us.
Priest
Our Father.

4 That we may see Thee by faith, and | live | through | Thee,
6 That through the power of the Comforter Thou | wouldest a- | bide with | us,
8 That Thou wouldest draw all men | un- | to | Thee,
10 That Thou wouldest endue the Clergy with the Spirit of power and love, and | of a | sound | mind,
12 That Thou wouldest stir up all Thy people to love | and to | good | works,
14 That Thou wouldest shortly accomplish the number of Thine elect and | hasten | Thy | kingdom,

We beseech Thee to hear us.

Priest

Let us pray.

GRANT, we beseech Thee, Almighty God, that like as we do believe Thy Only-begotten Son our Lord Jesus Christ to have ascended into the heavens; so we may also in heart and mind thither ascend, and with Him continually dwell, Who liveth and reigneth with Thee and the Holy Ghost, One God, world without end.

Choir

A - men.

Whitsuntide

LITANY OF THE HOLY GHOST

Priest or Two Cantors
Lord, have mercy up - on us.
Choir
Christ, have mercy up - on us.
Priest
Lord, have mercy up - on us.
Priest
O God the Father, of Hea - ven,
Choir
Have mer - cy up - on us.
O God the Son, Redeemer of the | world,
O God the Holy Ghost, the | Com-forter,
Holy Trinity, | One God,
O Holy Spirit, proceeding from the Father | and-the Son,
Spirit Who testifiest of | Christ,
Spirit of truth, Who teachest us | all things,
Spirit of the Lord, who fillest the | world,
Spirit of God, Who dwellest | in us,
Spirit of wisdom and under- | stan-ding,
Spirit of counsel and | ghostly strength,
Spirit of knowledge and true | god-liness,
Have mercy upon us.
Spirit of the fear of the | Lord,
Spirit of grace and | mer-cy,
Spirit of holiness and | pray-er,
Spirit of power and of a | sound mind,
Spirit of love, joy, and | peace,
Spirit of long-suffering and | gentle-ness,
Spirit of goodness and | faith,
Spirit of truth and | pa-tience,
Spirit of meekness and | tem-perance,
Spirit of modesty and | chas-tity,
Spirit of contrition and true re- | pen-tance,
Spirit Who helpest our in- | fir-mities,
Have mercy upon us.
Priest
Be merciful to us.
Choir
Holy Spirit, spare us.
Priest
Be merciful to us.
Choir
Holy Spirit, hear us.

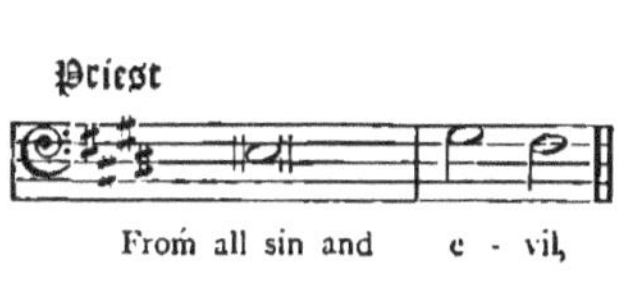
Priest
From all sin and e - vil,

Choir
Deliver us, O Ho - ly Spi - rit.

From the crafts and assaults of the | de-vil,
From all presumption and des- | pair,
From all hardness of | heart,
From pride and | van-ity,
From hatred and con- | ten-tion,
From all uncleanness of mind and | bo-dy,
From envy and | strife,
From anger and re- | venge,
From sloth and the love of | ease,
From deceit and | ly-ing,
From unbelief and | blas-phemy,
From every evil | spi-rit,

Deliver us, O Holy Spirit.

By Thy eternal procession from the Father | and-the Son,
By Thy work in the miraculous conception and birth of Jesus | Christ,
By Thy descent on Christ at His | Bap-tism,
By Thy appearance at the Transfigu | ra-tion,
By Thy coming down on the Day of | Pen-tecost,

Deliver us, O Holy Spirit.

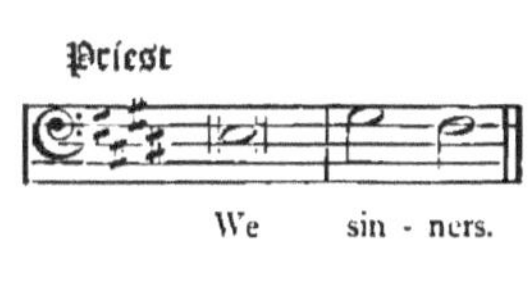
Priest
We sin - ners.

Choir
We be - seech Thee to hear us.

That Thou mayest | spare us,
That as we live in Thee, we may also walk | in Thee,
That by Thee we may mortify the deeds of the | bo-dy,
That we grieve not Thee the Holy Spirit of | God,
That we may be careful to keep the unity of Thy Church in the bond of | peace,
That we may remember that our bodies are Thy | tem-ples,
That walking in Thee we may not fulfil the lusts of the | flesh,
That Thou wouldest vouchsafe to make us meek and | gen-tle,

We beseech Thee to hear us.

That Thou wouldest vouchsafe to create in us the hunger and thirst after true | right-eousness,
That Thou wouldest vouchsafe to pour into our hearts sincere affections of mercy and | cha-rity,
That Thou wouldest vouchsafe to make us a clean heart and renew a right spirit with- | in us,
That we may be peacemakers, and worthy to be called the children of | God,
That Thou wouldest grant us to persevere unto the end in faith, hope, and | cha-rity,

We beseech Thee to hear us.

Priest
O Lamb of God, That tak - est a - way the sins of the world,
Org. Sw. Diaps.
Choir
Pour on us Thy Ho - ly Spi - - rit.
Priest
O Lamb of God, That tak - est a - way the sins of the world,
Org. Sw. Diaps.
Choir
Send forth upon us the prom - is'd Spi - rit of the Fa - - ther.

Priest
O Lamb of God, That tak - est a - way the sins of the world,
Org. *Sw. Diaps.*
Choir
pp
Grant un - to us the Spi - rit of peace.
pp
Priest
Our Father.
Priest
℣ When Thou lettest Thy Breath go forth they shall be made.
Choir
℟ And Thou shalt re - new the face of the earth.
Priest
Let us pray.
Choir
A - men.

GOD, Who (as at this time) didst teach the hearts of Thy faithful people, by the sending to them the light of Thy Holy Spirit; grant us by the Same Spirit to have a right judgment in all things, and evermore to rejoice in His holy comfort; through the merits of Christ Jesus our Saviour, Who liveth and reigneth with Thee, in the unity of the Same Spirit, One God, world without end.

Litany of the Holy Name of Jesus

Choir—*In unison*
Priest or Two Cantors
LORD, have mercy up - on us.
CHRIST, have mer-cy up - on us.
Priest
LORD, have mer-cy up - on us.
Choir
Priest
O CHRIST, hear us.
O CHRIST, gra - cious-ly hear us.
Choir
Priest
O GOD the FA - THER, of Heaven,
Have mer - cy up - on us.

O GOD the SON, Re- | deem-er of the | world,
O GOD the | HŎ-LȲ | GHOST,
HOLY | TRINI-TY, Ŏnĕ | GOD,

JESU, | SON of the liv-ing | GOD,
JESU, Brightness of the | FA-THER's glŏ- | ry,
JESU, our | E-ver-last-ing | Light,
JESU, | King of glŏ- | ry,
JESU, | Sun of right-eous- | ness,
JESU, Son of the | Vir-gin Mă- | ry,
JESU, | worthy of ăll | love,
JESU, Whose | Name is Won-der- | ful,
JESU, the | migh-tȳ | GOD,
JESU, the ever- | last-ing Fă- | ther,
JESU, the | Prĭnce ŏf | peace,
JESU, | mŏst Mĭgh- | ty,
JESU, | mŏst Pă- | tient,
JESU, | most o-bē- | dient,
JESU, Meek and | Lŏw-ly of | heart,
JESU, | Lover of chas-ti- | ty,
JESU, | our Be-lŏv- | ed,

Have mercy upon us.

JESU, | Au-thor of our | life,
JESU, | Pat-tern of all | virtues,
JESU, | Lov-er ŏf | souls,
JESU, | ŏur GŎD,
JESU, | ŏur Rĕ- | fuge,
JESU, | Fa-ther of the | poor,
JESU, | Trea-sure of the | faithful,
JESU, the | gŏŏd Shĕp- | herd,
JESU, the | trŭĕ Lĭght,
JESU, e- | ter-nal Wĭs- | dom,
JESU, | in-finite Gŏŏd- | ness,
JESU, the Way, the | Trŭth, and the | Life,
JESU, | Joy of Ăn- | gels,
JESU, | King of Pa-tri- | archs,
JESU, In- | spirer of Prŏ- | phets,
JESU, | Mas-ter of A- | postles,
JESU, | Teach-er of E- | vangelists,
JESU, | Strength of Măr- | tyrs,
JESU, | Lĭght of Con- | fessors,
JESU, | Spouse of Vĭr- | gins,
JESU, | Crŏwn ŏf | Saints,

Have mercy upon us.

Choir
Priest
Be merciful to us.
Spare us, Good Lord.
Choir
Priest
Be merciful to us.
Gra - cious - ly hear us.
Choir
Priest
From all e - vil,
Je - su, de - liv - er us.

From | all sin,
From | Thy wrath,
From the snares | of the de-vil,
From the lusts | of the flesh,
From ever- | last-ing death,
From neglect of Thy holy | in-spi-ra-tions,

By the mystery of Thy holy | In-car-na-tion,
By | Thy Na-ti-vity,
By Thy di- | vine Child-hood,
By Thy | sa-cred Life,
By | Thy La-bours,
By Thine Agony and | Blood-y Sweat,
By Thy | Cross and Pas-sion,
By Thy | Pains and Sor-rows,
By Thy | Death and Bu-rial,
By Thy glorious | Re-sur-rec-tion,
By Thy wonderful | As-cen-sion,
By Thy | ho-ly Joys,
By Thy | heav'n-ly Glo-ry,

Jesu, deliver us.

Priest
O Lamb of God, That tak - est a - way the sins of the world,
Org. Sw. Diaps.
Ped.
Choir
O Je - su, spare . . . us.
Priest
O Lamb of God, That tak - est a - way the sins of the world,
Org. Sw. Diaps.
Ped.
Choir
O Je - su, gra - cious - ly hear . . . us.

Priest
O LAMB of GOD, That tak - est a - way the sins of the world,
ORG. Sw. Diaps.
Ped.
Choir
O JE - SU, have mer - cy up - on . . . us.

Priest
O JE - SU, hear us.
Choir
O JE - SU, gra-cious-ly hear us.

Priest
Let us pray.

O GOD, the Strength of all them that put their trust in Thee, mercifully accept our prayers; and because through the weakness of our mortal nature we can do no good thing without Thee, grant us the help of Thy grace, that in keeping of Thy commandments we may please Thee, both in will and deed; through JESUS CHRIST our LORD.

Choir
A - men.

Litany for Saints' Days

Choir
Priest or Two Cantors
LORD, have mer-cy up - on us.
CHRIST, have mer - cy up - on us.
Priest
LORD, have mer - cy up - on us.
Choir
Priest
O CHRIST, hear us.
O CHRIST, gra-cious-ly hear us.
Choir
Priest
O GOD the FATHER, of Hea - ven.
Have mer - cy up - on us.

O GOD the SON, Redeemer of the | wörld,
O GOD the | HOLY GHOST,
HOLY TRINITY, | One GOD,

Have mercy upon us.

O LORD JESU, Who didst choose the Blessed Virgin Mary to be Thy | Mo-ther,
Thou Who dost send Thy Angels to do Thy | plea-sure,
Thou Who didst send John the Baptist to prepare Thy way be- | fore Thee,
Thou who didst put Thy words into the mouth of Thy holy Patriarchs and | Pro-phets,
Thou Who didst endue Thy twelve Apostles with singular gifts of the | HOLY GHOST,
Thou Who didst inspire and guide Thy holy E- | van-gelists,
Thou Who didst teach Thy Dis- | ci-ples,
Thou Who hast made Infants to glorify Thee by their | dêaths,
Thou Who didst strengthen Thy holy | Mar-tyrs,
Thou Who didst enable Thy Confessors boldly to confess Thee be- | fore men,
Thou Who didst enlighten the Doctors of the | Chûrch,
Thou Who didst give grace to all holy Priests and | Bi-shops,
Thou Who art glorified in | Thy Saints,
Thou Who art the joy and exceeding great reward of | Thy Saints,

Have mercy upon us.

Priest
Be mer - ci - ful to us,
Choir
And spare us, O Lord.
Priest
Be mer - ci - ful to us,
Choir
And gra - cious - ly hear us, O Lord.
Priest
From all pride,
Choir
Good Lord, de - liv - er us.

From all | covet-ous-ness,
From impurity and | all un-cleanness,
From envious and | bit-ter thoughts,
From | self in-dulgence,
From envy, anger, | and hatred,
From spiritual sloth and | all luke-warmness,
From walking in the | ways of sin,
By the mystery of Thy holy | In-car-nation,
By Thy Na- | ti-vi-ty,
By Thy Baptism and | ho-ly Fast,
By Thy | Cross and Passion,
By Thy | Death and Burial,
By Thy holy | Re-sur-rection,
By Thy wonderful As- | cen-sion,
By the Coming of the | Ho-ly Ghost,
In the | Day of judgment,

Good Lord, deliver us.

Priest
We sin - ners,
Choir
We be - seech Thee to hear us.

That we may | do Thy will,
That we may follow the blessed steps of Thy most | ho-ly life,
That we may always serve Thee in pureness of living | and truth,
That we may daily be renewed by Thy | Ho-ly Spirit,
That Thou wouldest lift up our minds to | heav'n-ly desires,
That we may never be ashamed to con- | fess Thy Name,
That we may be aided by the prayers of the | right-eous,
That we may follow the examples of | Thy Saints,
That we may reign with Thee in | glo-ry,
That Thou wouldest vouchsafe to all Thy faithful servants eternal | rest and peace,

We beseech Thee to hear us.

Priest
Son of God,
Choir
We be-seech Thee to hear us.
Priest
O Lamb of God, That tak - est a - way the sins of the world,
Choir
Spare us, O Lord.
Priest
O Lamb of God, That tak - est a - way the sins of the world,
Choir
Gra - cious - ly hear us, O Lord.
Priest
O Lamb of God, That tak - est a - way the sins of the world,
Choir
Have mer - cy up - on us.

Priest
O CHRIST, hear us.
Choir
O CHRIST, gra-cious-ly hear us.
Priest
LORD, have mer - cy up - on us.
Choir
CHRIST, have mer - cy up - on us.
Priest
LORD, have mer - cy up - on us.
Priest
Our FATHER.
Priest
℣ All Thy works praise Thee, O LORD.
Choir
℟ And Thy Saints give thanks un - to Thee.
Priest
Let us pray.
Choir
A - men.

O ALMIGHTY GOD, Who hast knit together Thine elect in one communion and fellowship, in the mystical Body of Thy SON CHRIST our LORD; grant us grace so to follow Thy blessed Saints, in all virtuous and godly living, that we may come to those unspeakable joys, which Thou hast prepared for them that unfeignedly love Thee; through JESUS CHRIST our LORD.

Litany of the Holy Angels

Priest or Two Cantors
Lord, have mer - cy up - on us.
Choir
Christ, have mer - cy up - on us.
Priest
Lord, have mer - cy up - on us.
Priest
O Christ, hear us.
Choir
O Christ, gra - cious - ly hear us.
Priest
O God the Father, of Heaven.
Choir
Have mer - cy up - on us.

O God the Son, Redeemer | of the | world,
O God the | Ho-ly | Ghost,
Holy Trinity, | One | God,

O GOD, Who hast made Angels and men to | do Thee | service,
Thou Who dost send Thy Angels to minister to those who shall be heirs | of sal- | vation,
Thou Who by Thy Angels didst lead forth Lot from the | midst of | sinners,
Thou Who by Thy Angels didst give the | law to | Moses,
Thou Who by Thy Angels didst bring the joyful tidings of the | birth of | Christ,
Thou Who by Thy Angels didst minister to Jesus in the | wil-der- | ness,

Have mercy upon us.

Thou Who by Thy Angels didst carry Lazarus to | A-braham's | bosom,
Thou Who by Thy Angel didst strengthen Jesus in His | a-go- | ny,
Thou Who didst bid Thy Angels to watch at the | tomb of | Jesus,
Thou Who didst send Thy Angels to proclaim the As- | cension of | Jesus,
Thou Whose Angels will be present at the | last | judgment,
Thou Who by Thy Angels wilt separate the evil | from the | good,
Thou Who by Thy Angels dost sup- | port the | dying,
Thou Who by Thy Angels dost bear to Heaven the souls | of the | righteous,

Have mercy upon us.

Priest
Be merciful to us,
Choir
And spare us
Priest
Be merciful to us,
Choir
And graciously hear us.
Priest
From all dangers, by Thy Holy An-gels,
Choir
Good LORD, de - liver us.
Priest
We sin - ners,
Choir
We be - seech Thee to hear us.

From the snares of the | de-vil,
From famine, war, and | pes-tilence,
From a sudden and unpre- | pared death.
} *Good LORD, deliver us.*

That Thou wouldest | spare | us,
That Thou wouldest be merciful | to | us,
That Thou wouldest vouchsafe to govern and preserve Thy | ho-ly | Church,
That Thou wouldest vouchsafe to bless all the Bishops | of the | Church,
That Thou wouldest vouchsafe to bestow peace and unity upon all | Chris-tian | princes,
That it may please Thee to give Thine Angels charge | o-ver | us,
That it may please Thee to fill us with love for those | glo-rious | spirits,
That it may please Thee by the ministry of Thy Angels to keep us in | all our | ways,
That it may please Thee that after our death the Angels may carry our souls into | Thy | rest,
} *We beseech Thee to hear us.*

Priest
O Lamb of God, That takest away the sins of the world.
Org. Sw. Diaps.
Ped.
Choir
Spare us, O Lord.
Priest
O Lamb of God, That takest away the sins of the world.
[Accompaniment as before]
Choir
Hear us, O Lord.
Priest
O Lamb of God, That takest away the sins of the world.
[Accompaniment as before]
Choir
Have mer - cy up - on us.

Priest
LORD, have mer - cy up - on us.
Choir
CHRIST, have mer - cy up - on us.

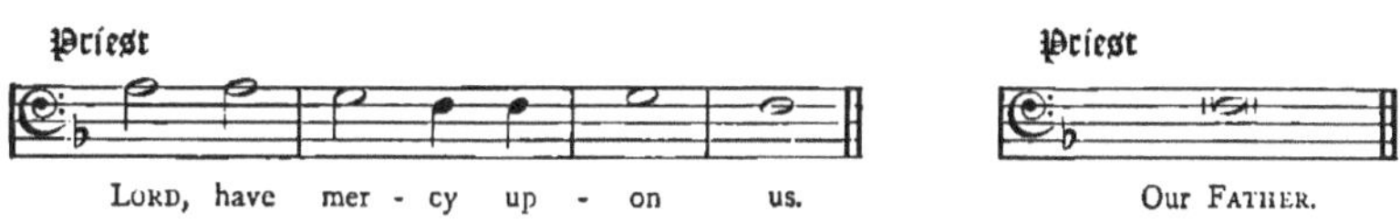
Priest
LORD, have mer - cy up - on us.
Priest
Our FATHER.

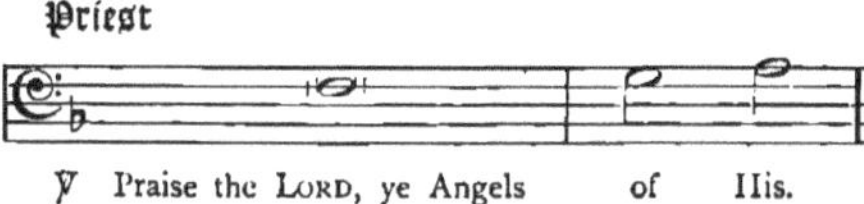
Priest
℣ Praise the LORD, ye Angels of His.

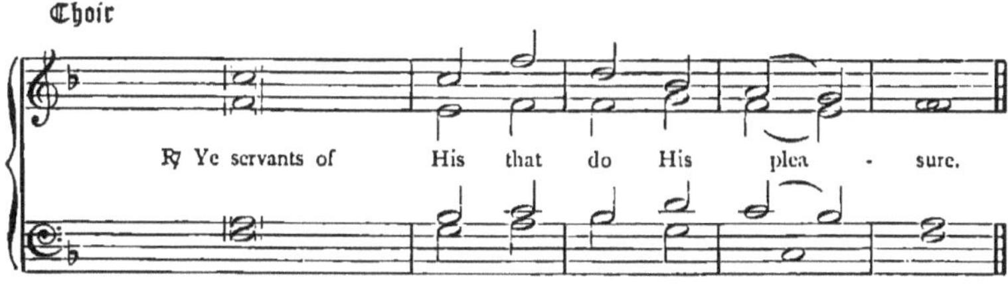
Choir
℟ Ye servants of His that do His plea - sure.

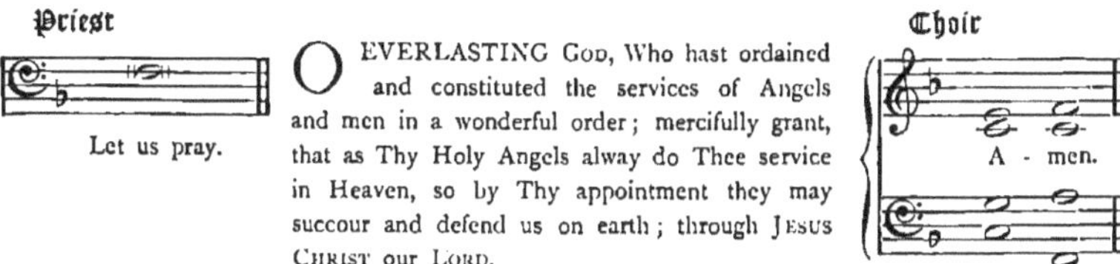
Priest
Let us pray.
Choir
A - men.

O EVERLASTING GOD, Who hast ordained and constituted the services of Angels and men in a wonderful order; mercifully grant, that as Thy Holy Angels alway do Thee service in Heaven, so by Thy appointment they may succour and defend us on earth; through JESUS CHRIST our LORD.

Litany for the Church

Priest or Two Cantors
Lord, have mer - cy up - on us.
Choir
Christ, have mer - cy up - on us.
Priest
Lord, have mer - cy up - on us.
Priest
O Christ, hear us.
Choir
O Christ, gra - cious - ly hear us.
Priest
O God the Father, of Heaven,
Choir
Have mer - cy up - on us.

O God the Son, Redeemer | of the | world,
O God the | Ho-ly | Ghost,
Holy Trinity, | One | God,

Have mercy upon us.

O God, Who didst choose the Church before the foundation | of the | world,
Thou Who hast built Thy Church on the foundation of the Apostles and | Pro- | phets,
Thou Who lovedst Thy Church and gavest Thyself | for | it,
Thou Who hast promised to be with her always even unto the end | of the | world,
Thou Who hast promised that the gates of hell shall not prevail a- | gainst | her,
Thou Who dost call the Church Thine own | Bo- | dy,
Thou Who art not far from every | one of | us,
Thou Who hast not left Thyself without a | wit- | ness,
Thou Who willest that all men should be saved, and come to the knowledge | of the | truth,
Thou Who hast not cast away Thy people | Is-ra- | el,
Thou Who art long-suffering to us-ward, not willing that any should | pe- | rish,
Thou Who ever livest to make intercession | for | us,

Have mercy upon us.

Priest
Be gracious to us,
Choir
And spare us, O Lord.

Choir
Priest
Good LORD, de - li - ver us.
From all sin and e - - - vil,

From all ignorance and | un-be- | lief,
From all blindness | of | heart,
From all false doctrine, heresy, | and | schism,
From our unhappy di- | vi- | sions,
Good LORD, deliver us.

Priest
By Thine Ascension in - to Heaven.

By Thine Enthronement at the right | hand of | GOD,
By Thine Almighty | In-ter- | cession,
By Thy | ten-der | Love,
By the Multitude of Thy | mer- | cies,
Good LORD, deliver us.

Choir
Priest
We be-seech Thee to hear us, Good LORD.
We sin - ners,

That Thou wouldest pour down Thy SPIRIT | on Thy | Church,
That Thou wouldest grant her unity, peace, and | true | con-cord,
That Thou wouldest endue Thy Priests with the spirit of power and love, and of a | sound | mind,
That Thou wouldest give them more abundantly the graces of courage, faithfulness, and | fer-vent | zeal,
That it may please Thee to preserve them in all dangers of their | souls and | bo-dies,
That Thou wouldest bless all home and | for-eign | Miss-ions,
That it may please Thee to send forth labourers | into Thine | har-vest,
We beseech Thee to hear us, Good LORD.

That it may please Thee to make them shine as lights | in the | world,
That it may please Thee to convert all heathen and | un-be- | lie-vers,
That it may please Thee to turn many to | right-eous- | ness,
That it may please Thee to bring all into the | way of | truth,
That the heart of Israel may turn unto the LORD, and the vail be | taken a- | way,
That the earth may be full of the knowledge of the LORD, as the waters | cover the | sea,
That Thou wouldest be pleased shortly to accomplish the number of Thine elect, and to | hasten Thy | King-dom,
We beseech Thee to hear us, Good LORD.

Choir
Priest
We be - seech Thee to hear us.
SON of GOD,

Priest
O Lamb of God, That tak-est a - way the sins of the world,
Org. Sw. Diaps.
Choir
Have mer - cy up - on us.
Priest
O Lamb of God, That tak - est a - way the sins of the world,
[Accompaniment as before]
Choir
Hear us, O Lord.
Priest
O Lamb of God, That tak - est a - way the sins of the world,
[Accompaniment as before]
Choir
pp
Grant us Thy peace. . . .
pp

Priest
O Christ, hear us.
Choir
O Christ, gra - cious - ly hear us.
Priest
Lord, have mer - cy up - on us.
Choir
Christ, have mer - cy up - on us.
Priest
Lord, have mer - cy up - on us.
Priest
Our Father.
Priest
O pray for the peace of Je - ru - sa - lem.
Priest
They shall pros - per That love Thee.
Priest
Let us pray.
Choir
A - - men.

LORD, we beseech Thee to keep Thy household the Church in continual godliness; that through Thy protection it may be free from all adversities, and devoutly given to serve Thee in good works, to the glory of Thy Name; through JESUS CHRIST our LORD.

Litany of the Blessed Sacrament

Priest or Two Cantors
LORD, have mer - cy up - on us.
Choir
CHRIST, have mer - cy up - on us.
Priest
LORD, have mer - cy up - on us.
Priest
O CHRIST, hear us.
Choir
O CHRIST, gra - cious - ly hear us.
Priest
O GOD the FATHER, of Heaven,
Choir
Have mer - cy up - on us.
Priest
JESU, GOD . . . and Man,
Choir
Have mer - cy up - on us.

O GOD the SON, Redeemer | of the | world,
O GOD the | HO-LY | GHOST,
HOLY TRINITY, | One | GOD,
Have mercy upon us.

JESU, Who before Thy Passion didst desire to eat this Passover with | Thy dis- | ci- | ples,
JESU, Who when Thou wert about to institute this holy Sacrament didst first wash | Thy dis- | ci-ples' | feet,
JESU, Priest for ever, Who didst offer Thyself as a Victim upon the | al-tar of the | Cross,
JESU, Who dost vouchsafe to be present among us under the | forms of | bread and | wine,
JESU, the Bread of life, Who | cam-est | down from | Heaven,
Have mercy upon us.

JESU, the heavenly Manna, Who dost nourish Thy elect in the | de-sert | of this | world,
JESU, the Food of Angels, Whose sweetness fills our | hearts with | heaven-ly | joys,
JESU, the Lamb without spot, Who, having been once sacrificed, art continually presented before the FATHER as our Pro- | pi-ti- | ä- | tion,
JESU, Who didst make Thyself known to Thy two disciples in the | Break- | ing of | Bread,
Have mercy upon us.

JESU, Who dost feed us with Thy very | Bo-dy | and | Blood,
JESU, Who hast said, Come unto Me all ye that labour and are heavy laden, and | I will | give you | rest,
JESU, Who hadst compassion on the multitude | in the | wilder- | ness,
JESU, Who exhortest us to receive Thee, saying, My Flesh is meat indeed, and My | Blood is | drink in- | deed,
JESU, Who hast said, Except ye eat the Flesh of the SON of Man and drink His Blood ye | have no | life in | you,

Have mercy upon us.

JESU, Who hast said, He that eateth My Flesh and drinketh My Blood dwelleth in Me, and | I | in | him,
JESU, Who hast said, Whoso eateth My Flesh and drinketh My Blood | hath e- | ter-nal | life,
JESU, Who, giving Thyself to be our Meat and Drink, didst say, This is My Body which is given for you, this is My Blood | which is | shed for | you,
JESU, Who in this august and venerable Mystery art Thyself both | Priest and | Vic- | tim,
JESU, Who in this wonderful Sacrament hast left us a Memorial | of Thy | Pas- | sion,

Have mercy upon us.

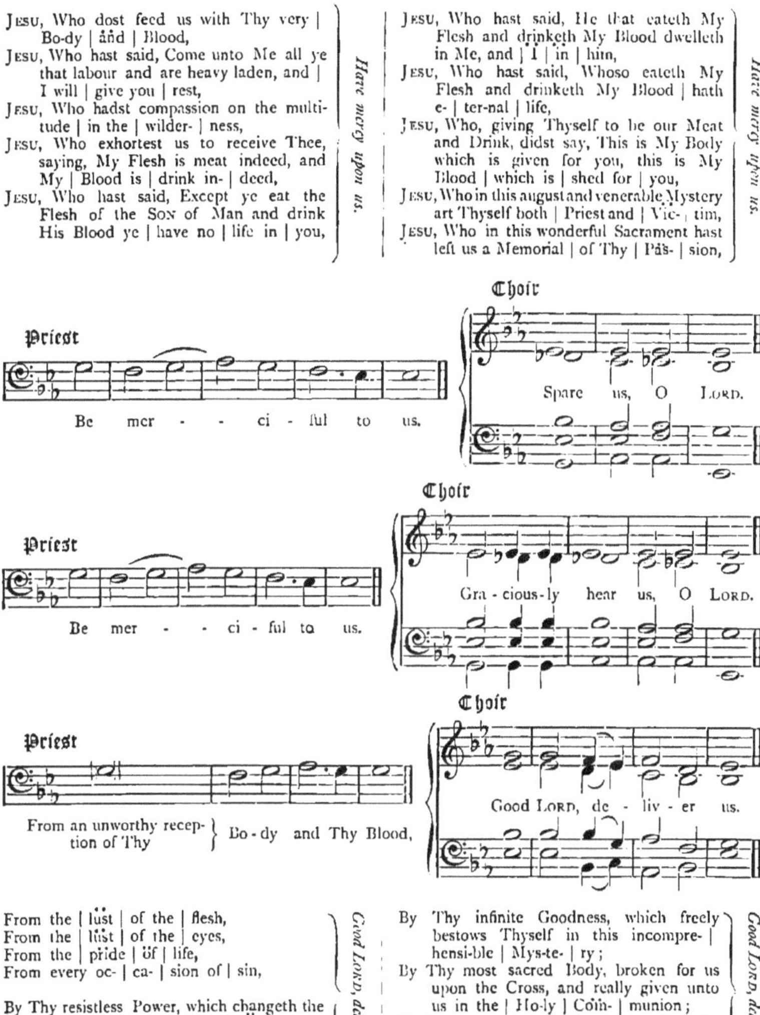
Choir
Priest
Be mer - - ci - ful to us.
Spare us, O LORD.
Choir
Priest
Be mer - - ci - ful to us.
Gra - cious - ly hear us, O LORD.
Choir
Priest
From an unworthy reception of Thy Bo - dy and Thy Blood,
Good LORD, de - liv - er us.

From the | lust | of the | flesh,
From the | lust | of the | eyes,
From the | pride | of | life,
From every oc- | ca- | sion of | sin,

By Thy resistless Power, which changeth the course of nature | as Thou | will- | est,
By Thy unsearchable Wisdom, which disposeth all things in | per-fect | or- | der,

Good LORD, deliver us.

By Thy infinite Goodness, which freely bestows Thyself in this incompre- | hensi-ble | Mys-te- | ry;
By Thy most sacred Body, broken for us upon the Cross, and really given unto us in the | Ho-ly | Com- | munion;
By Thy most precious Blood, poured out for us upon the Cross, and really given to us in the | Cup of | bless- | ing;

Good LORD, deliver us.

Priest
We sin - - - - - ners,
Choir
We be - seech Thee to hear us.
That it may please Thee to preserve and increase our faith, reverence, and devotion towards this | won-drous | Sa-cra- | ment,
That it may please Thee to enable us through a true confession of our sins worthily to receive the | Ho-ly | Eu-cha- | rist,
That it may please Thee to deliver us from all heresy, unbelief, and | hard- | ness of | heart,
We beseech Thee to hear us.
That it may please Thee to impart to us the precious and heavenly fruits of this most | ho-ly | Sa-cra- | ment,
That it may please Thee to strengthen and defend us with this heavenly food at the | hour | of our | death,
That as by faith we here adore Thee present although unseen, so we may hereafter behold Thee | face to | face in | Heaven,
We beseech Thee to hear us.
Priest
Son of . . . God,
Choir
We be - seech Thee to hear us.
Priest—Before each Response
Slow
O Lamb . of God, That tak - est a - way the sins of the world,
Slow
Org. Sw. Diaps.
Choir—First Response
pp
Spare us, O Lord.
pp
Choir—Second Response
p
Gra - cious - ly hear us, O Lord.
p

Priest
Slow
O LAMB of GOD, That takest away the sins of the world,
Slow
ORG. Sw. Diaps.
Choir—3rd Response
Have mer - cy up - on us.
Priest
O CHRIST, hear us.
Choir
O CHRIST, gra - cious-ly hear us.
Priest
℣ He {gave them / Food from} Hea-ven.
Choir
℟ So man did eat An - gels' Food.
Priest
Let us pray.
Choir
A - men.

O GOD, Who hast prepared for them that love Thee such good things as pass man's understanding; pour into our hearts such love toward Thee, that we, loving Thee above all things, may obtain Thy promises, which exceed all that we can desire; through JESUS CHRIST our LORD.

Litany of the Holy Child Jesus

Choir
Priest or Two Cantors
LORD, have mercy up - on us.
CHRIST, have mer - cy up - on . . . . us.
Priest
LORD, have mercy up - on us.
Choir
Priest
O GOD the FATHER, of Hea - ven,
Have mer - cy up - on . . . us.
O GOD the | SON, our | SA-VIOUR,
O GOD the HOLY GHOST, our | Sanc-ti- | fi-er,
HOLY TRINITY, | One | GOD,
JESU, | SON of | GOD,
JESU, | SON of | Ma-ry,
JESU, equal | to Thy | FA-THER,
JESU, subject | to Thy | Mo-ther,
JESU, | Prince of | Peace
JESU, | Hope of | Saints,
JESU, | Refuge of | sin-ners,
JESU, First-born of | all | crea-tures,
Have mercy upon us.
JESU, made | Man | for us,
JESU, | born in a | sta-ble,
JESU, | laid in a | man-ger,
JESU, obedient | to Thy | pa-rents,
JESU, Who didst | love the | poor,
JESU, Who didst | suffer in | si-lence,
JESU, Who didst | love | chil-dren,
JESU, Who didst | die on the | Cross,
JESU, Who sittest at the right | hand of | GOD,
JESU, Who art present in the Blessed Sacrament under the forms of | Bread and | Wine,
Have mercy upon us.
Choir
Priest
By Thy hum - ble birth.
LORD JE - SU, streng - then us.
By Thy | Cold and | Hun-ger,
By | Thy | tears,
By | Thy | Sor-rows,
By | Thy | Po-verty,
By | Thy | La-bour,
By | Thine | A-gony,
By Thy | Sweat of | Blood,
LORD JESU, strengthen us.
By Thy | Crown of | thorns,
By Thy | Cross and | Pass-ion,
By Thy | Death and | Bu-rial,
By Thy glorious | Re-sur- | rec-tion,
By Thy triumphant | As- | cen-sion,
By Thy Life that | ne-ver | ends,
By Thy | Love for | chil-dren,
LORD JESU, strengthen us.

Priest
O LAMB of GOD, That takest away the sins of the world,
Choir
Spare us, O LORD.
Priest
O LAMB of GOD, That takest away the sins of the world,
Choir
Hear us, O LORD.
Priest
O LAMB of GOD, That takest away the sins of the world,
Choir
Have mer - cy on us.
Priest
Our FATHER.
Priest
Let us pray.
Choir
A - men.

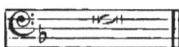

ALMIGHTY GOD, Who hast given us Thy Only-begotten SON to take our nature upon Him, and (as at this time) to be born of a pure Virgin; grant that we, being regenerate, and made Thy children by adoption and grace, may daily be renewed by Thy HOLY SPIRIT; through the Same our LORD JESUS CHRIST, Who liveth and reigneth with Thee and the Same SPIRIT, ever One GOD, world without end.

Litany for a Happy Death

Choir
Priest or Two Cantors
Lord, have mercy upon us.
Christ, have mercy upon us.
Priest
Lord, have mer - cy up - on us.
Choir
Priest
O Christ, hear us.
O Christ, graciously hear us.
Choir
Priest
O God the Father, of Heaven,
Have mer - cy up - on us.

O God the Son, Re- | deem-er | of the | world,
O God the Ho- | ly Ghost,
Holy | Trini-ty | One | God,

O GOD, Who in Thine own Image didst | make man,
Thou Who didst breathe into his nostrils the breath | of | life,
Thou Who madest not death, neither hast pleasure in the destruction | of the | liv- | ing,
Thou Who didst promise a portion in Thy Kingdom to the | pen-i- | tent thief,
Thou Who for our sakes became obedient unto death, even the death | of the | Cross,

Have mercy upon us.

Thou Who when dying didst commend Thy Spirit into the hands | of Thy | Fa- | ther,
Thou Who through death didst destroy him that | had the | power of | death,
Thou Who wast wounded for our transgressions, and bruised for | our in- | i-qui- | ties,
Thou Who dost wipe away all | tears | from the | eyes,
Thou Who hast | power of | life and | death,
Thou Who wilt have all men to be | sa- | ved,
Thou Who shalt come to judge the | quick | and the | dead,

Have mercy upon us.

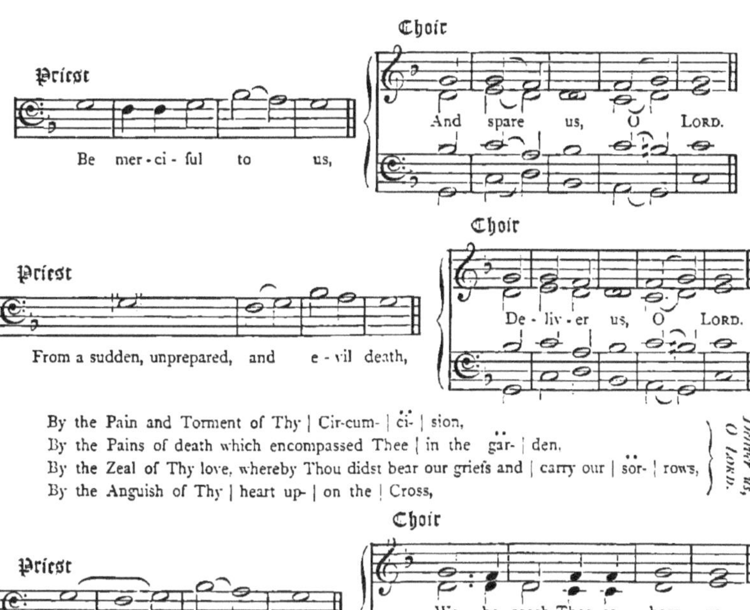

Priest
Be mer-ci-ful to us,
Choir
And spare us, O LORD.
Priest
From a sudden, unprepared, and e-vil death,
Choir
De-liv-er us, O LORD.

By the Pain and Torment of Thy | Cir-cum- | ci- | sion,
By the Pains of death which encompassed Thee | in the gar- | den,
By the Zeal of Thy love, whereby Thou didst bear our griefs and | carry our | sor- | rows,
By the Anguish of Thy | heart up- | on the | Cross,

Deliver us, O LORD.

Priest

We . . . sin - ners,

Choir

We be-seech Thee to hear us.

That we may confess that we are strangers and | pil-grims | on the earth,
That having here no continuing city, we may | seek | one to | come,
That Thou wouldest not deal with us | af-ter | our | sins,
That our light affliction which is but for a moment, may work in us an eternal | weight of | glo- | ry,
That looking unto JESUS, we may run with patience the race that is | set be- | fore | us,
That we put not off the day | of sal- | va- | tion,
That we serve Thee without fear, in holiness and righteousness, all the | days of | our | life,

We beseech Thee to hear us.

That to us to live may be CHRIST, | and to | die | gain,
That though we walk through the valley of the shadow of death, we may fear no | e- | vil,
That we may die the | death | of the | righteous,
That Thou wouldest lighten our eyes, that we | sleep | not in | death,
That Thou wouldest bring our souls out of prison, that we may give thanks un-to | Thy | Name,
That when we are dying, Thou wouldest comfort us as Thou didst the | pen-i- | tent | thief,
That we may hasten to enter into that rest which we | hope for | in | heaven.

We beseech Thee to hear us.

Priest
Son . . . of God,
Choir
We be - seech Thee to hear us.
Priest
O Lamb of God, That takest away the sins of the world,
Choir
Have mer - cy up - on us.
Priest
O Lamb of God, That takest away the sins of the world,
Choir
Have mer - cy up - on us.
Priest
O Lamb of God, That takest away the sins of the world,
Choir
p
Grant us Thy peace.

Choir
Priest
O CHRIST, hear us,
O CHRIST, graciously hear us.
Choir
Priest
LORD, have mercy upon us.
CHRIST, have mercy upon us.
Priest
LORD, have mer - cy up - on us.
Priest
Our FATHER.
Priest
℣ Thou hast been our suc - cour.
Choir
℟ Leave us not, neither forsake us, O GOD of our sal - va - tion.

Priest

Let us pray.

ALMIGHTY and Merciful GOD, of Whose only gift it cometh that Thy faithful people do unto Thee true and laudable service; grant, we beseech Thee, that we may so faithfully serve Thee in this life, that we fail not finally to attain Thy heavenly promises; through the merits of JESUS CHRIST our LORD.

Choir

A - men.

An Evening Service

(*Taken from the Bible and Prayer Book*)

Priest or Two Cantors
In the Name of the FATHER, and of the SON, and of the HOLY GHOST. A - men.
Priest
BLESSING
Choir
The LORD bless us, and keep us; the LORD lift up the light of His countenance upon us, and give us peace, now and for
e - ver- more.
A - men.
Priest
THE SHORT LESSON
Be sober, be vigilant; because your adversary the devil, as a roaring lion, walketh about, seeking whom he may devour; whom resist steadfast
in the faith.
Choir
Priest
℟ Thanks be to GOD.
℣ But Thou, O LORD, have mercy up - on us.
Choir
Priest
Priest
℟ Who hath made Heaven and earth.
℣ Our help is in the Name
of the LORD.
Our FATHER.

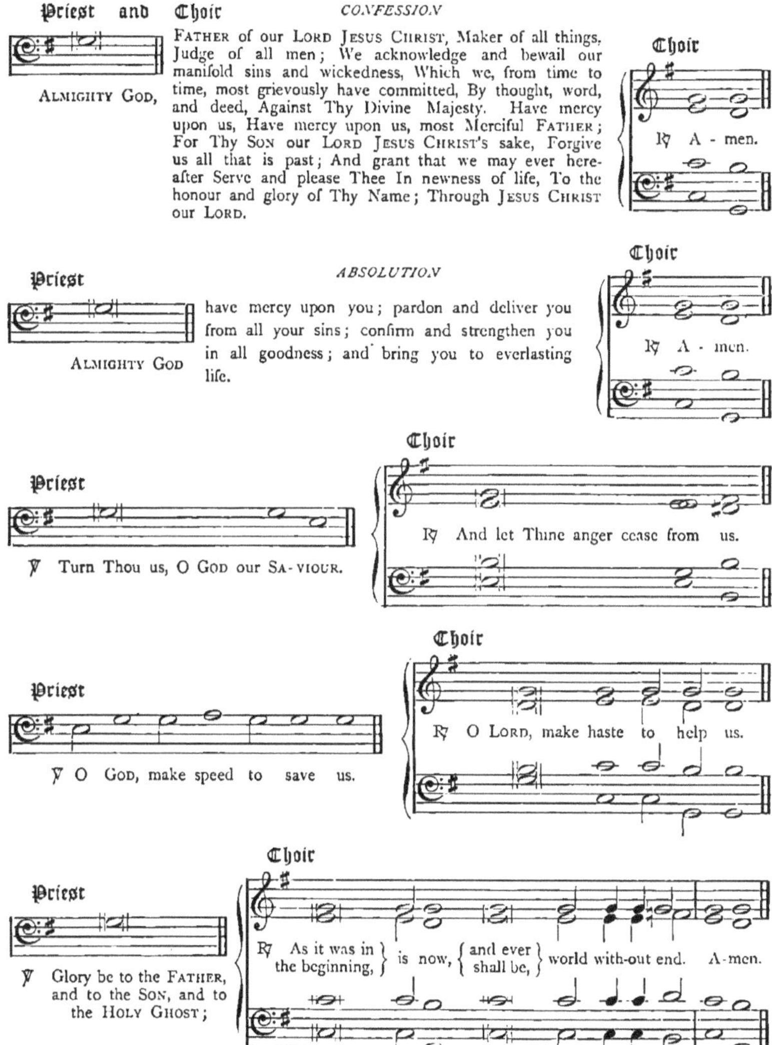
Priest and Choir
CONFESSION
ALMIGHTY GOD,
FATHER of our LORD JESUS CHRIST, Maker of all things, Judge of all men; We acknowledge and bewail our manifold sins and wickedness, Which we, from time to time, most grievously have committed, By thought, word, and deed, Against Thy Divine Majesty. Have mercy upon us, Have mercy upon us, most Merciful FATHER; For Thy SON our LORD JESUS CHRIST'S sake, Forgive us all that is past; And grant that we may ever hereafter Serve and please Thee In newness of life, To the honour and glory of Thy Name; Through JESUS CHRIST our LORD.
Choir
℟ A - men.
Priest
ABSOLUTION
ALMIGHTY GOD
have mercy upon you; pardon and deliver you from all your sins; confirm and strengthen you in all goodness; and bring you to everlasting life.
Choir
℟ A - men.
Priest
℣ Turn Thou us, O GOD our SA - VIOUR.
Choir
℟ And let Thine anger cease from us.
Priest
℣ O GOD, make speed to save us.
Choir
℟ O LORD, make haste to help us.
Priest
℣ Glory be to the FATHER, and to the SON, and to the HOLY GHOST;
Choir
℟ As it was in the beginning, is now, and ever shall be, world with-out end. A-men.

Priest ANTIPHON
Have mer - cy.
Priest ANTIPHON IN EASTER-TIDE
Al - le - lu - - - - - ia.

PSALM IV. Cum Invocarem

HEAR me, when I call, O God of my | right-eousness: Thou hast set me at liberty when I was in trouble; have mercy upon me, and hearken | unto my prayer.

2 O ye sons of men, how long will ye blaspheme Mine | hon-our: and have such pleasure in vanity, and seek | af-ter leas-ing?

3 Know this also, that the Lord hath chosen to Himself the man that is | god-ly: when I call upon the Lord | He will hear me.

4 Stand in awe, and | sin not: commune with your own heart, and in your chamber | and be still.

5 Offer the sacrifice of | right-eousness: and put your | trust in the Lord.

6 There be many that | say: Who will shew us | a-ny good?

7 Lord, lift Thou | up: the light of Thy counte- | nance up-on us.

8 Thou hast put gladness in my | heart: since the time that their corn, and wine, and | oil in-creas-ed.

9 I will lay me down in peace, and take my | rest: for it is Thou, Lord, only that makest me | dwell in safe-ty.

Glory be to the Father, and to the | Son: and to the | Ho-ly Ghost;

As it was in the beginning, is now, and ever | shall be: world without | end. A-men.

PSALM XXXI. In te, Domine, speravi

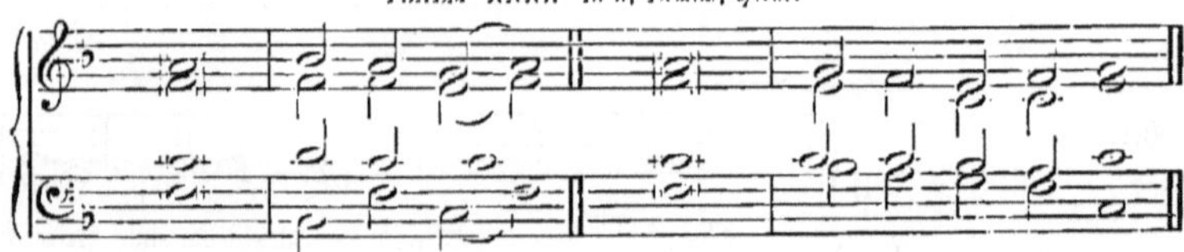

IN Thee, O Lord, have I | put my trust: let me never be put to confusion, deliver me | in Thy right-eous-ness.

2 Bow down Thine | ear to hear me: make haste | to de-liv-er me.

3 And be Thou my strong Rock, and | House of‿de-fence : that | Thou mayest save me.

4 For Thou art my strong Rock, | and my Cas-tle : be Thou also my Guide, and lead me | for Thy Name's sake.

5 Draw me out of the net, that they have laid | priv-ily for me : for | Thou art my Strength.

6 Into Thy hands I com- | mend my spi-rit : for Thou hast redeemed me, O | LORD, Thou GOD of truth.

Glory be to the FATHER, | and to‿the SON : and | to the HO-LY GHOST;

As it was in the beginning, is now, and | e-ver shall be : world without | end. A-men.

PSALM XCI. Qui habitat

WHOSO dwelleth under the defence | of‿the Most High : shall abide under the shadow | of the‿Al-migh-ty.

2 I will say unto the LORD, Thou art my Hope and | my Strong Hold : my GOD, in | Him will I trust.

3 For He shall deliver thee from the | snare of‿the hun-ter : and from the | noi-some pes-ti-lence.

4 He shall defend thee under His wings, and thou shalt be safe | under His fea-thers : His faithfulness and truth shall be thy | shield and buck-ler.

5 Thou shalt not be afraid for any | terror by night : nor for the arrow that | fli-eth by day.

6 For the pestilence that | walketh in dark-ness : nor for the sickness that destroyeth | in the noon-day.

7 A thousand shall fall beside thee, and ten thousand at | thy right hand : but it shall | not come nigh thee.

8 Yea, with thine eyes shalt | thou be-hold : and see the reward | of the‿un-god-ly.

9 For Thou, LORD, | art my Hope : Thou hast set Thine house of de- | fence ve-ry high.

10 There shall no evil happen | un-to thee : neither shall any plague come | nigh thy dwell-ing

11 For He shall give His Angels charge | o-ver thee : to | keep thee in‿all thy ways.

12 They shall bear thee | in their hands : that thou hurt not thy | foot a-gainst a stone.

13 Thou shalt go upon the | lion and ad-der : the young lion and the dragon shalt thou tread | un-der thy feet.

14 Because he hath set his love upon Me, therefore will | I de-liv-er‿him : I will set him up, because he hath | known My Name.

15 He shall call upon Me, and | I will hear him : yea, I am with him in trouble; I will deliver him, and bring | him to ho-nour.

16 With long life will I | sa-tis-fy him : and shew him | My sal-va-tion.

Glory be to the FATHER, | and to‿the SON : and | to the HO-LY GHOST;

As it was in the beginning, is now, and | e-ver shall be : world without | end. A-men.

PSALM CXXXIV. Ecce nunc

BEHOLD now, praise the | LORD : all ye | ser-vants of the Lord;

2 Ye that by night stand in the house of the | LORD : even in the courts of the | house of our GOD.

3 Lift up your hands in the | sanctuary : and | praise the LORD.

4 The LORD that made Heaven and | earth : give thee blessing | out of Si-on.

Glory be to the FATHER, and to the | SON : and to the | HO-LY GHOST;

As it was in the beginning, is now, and ever | shall be : world without | end. A-men.

Choir *ANTIPHON*

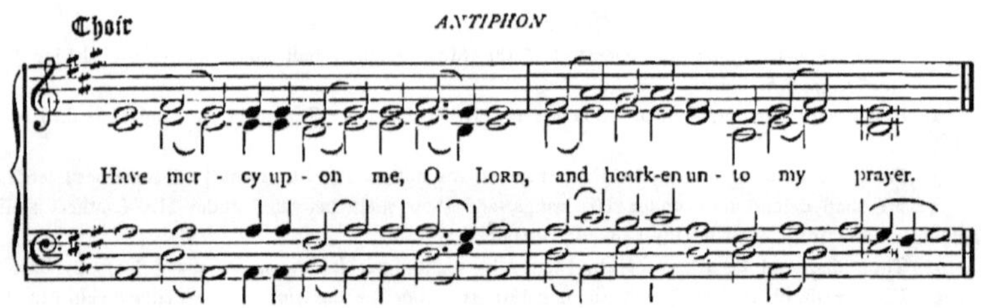
Have mer - cy up - on me, O LORD, and heark-en un - to my prayer.

Choir *ANTIPHON IN EASTER-TIDE*

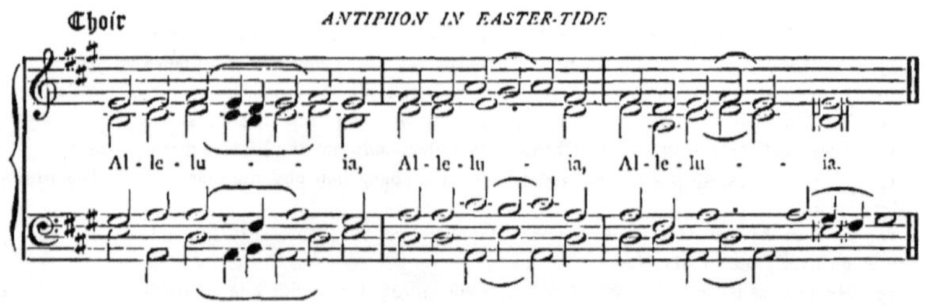
Al - le - lu - - ia, Al - le - lu - ia, Al - le - lu - - ia.

HYMN

Te lucis ante terminum

A - men.

BEFORE the ending of the day,
Creator of the world, we pray
That with Thy wonted favour, Thou
Wouldst be our Guard and Keeper now.

From all ill dreams defend our eyes,
From nightly fears and fantasies;
Tread under foot our ghostly foe,
That no pollution we may know.

O FATHER, that we ask be done,
Through JESUS CHRIST, Thine Only SON;
Who, with the HOLY GHOST and Thee,
Shall live and reign eternally. Amen.

Doxology during the Christmas Season

ALL honour, laud, and glory be:
O JESU, Virgin-born, to Thee.
All glory, as is ever meet,
To FATHER and to Paraclete. Amen.

Doxology during the Octave of the Epiphany

ALL glory, LORD, to Thee we pay,
For Thine Epiphany to-day:
All glory, as is ever meet,
To FATHER and to Paraclete. Amen.

Doxology in Easter-tide

TO Thee Who dead again dost live,
All glory, LORD, Thy people give:
All glory, as is ever meet,
To FATHER and to Paraclete. Amen.

Doxology in Ascension-tide

ALL glory, LORD, to Thee we pay,
Ascending o'er the stars to-day:
All glory, as is ever meet,
To FATHER and to Paraclete. Amen.

Doxology in Whitsun-tide

TO GOD the FATHER, GOD the SON,
And GOD the SPIRIT, praise be done,
And CHRIST the LORD upon us pour
The SPIRIT's gift for evermore. Amen.

Priest
THE CHAPTER
℣ Thou, O Lord, art in the midst of us, and we are called by Thy Name; leave us not, O Lord our God.
Choir
℟ Thanks be to God.
Priest
℣ Into Thy hands, O Lord, I commend my spi - rit.
ADD IN EASTER-TIDE
Alleluia, Al - le - lu - ia.
Choir
℟ For Thou hast redeemed me, O Lord, thou God of truth.
ADD IN EASTER-TIDE
Alleluia, Al - le - lu - ia.
Priest
℣ Glory be to the Father, and to the Son, and to the Ho - ly Ghost.
Choir
℟ Into Thy hands, O Lord, I commend my spi - rit.
ADD IN EASTER-TIDE
Alleluia, Al - le - lu - ia.
Priest
℣ Keep us, O Lord, as the apple of an eye.
ADD IN EASTER-TIDE
Al - le - lu - ia.
Choir
℟ Hide us under the shadow of Thy wings.
ADD IN EASTER-TIDE
Al - le - lu - ia.

Priest *ANTIPHON*

Come, O LORD.

NUNC DIMITTIS. S. LUKE ii. 29

LORD, now lettest Thou Thy servant de- | part in peace : according | to Thy Word.
For mine | eyes have seen : Thy Sal- | va-tion.
Which Thou | hast pre-par-ed : before the face of | all peo-ple ;
To be a light to | lighten the Gen-tiles : and to be the glory of Thy | peo-ple Is-rael.
Glory be to the FATHER, | and to the SON : and to the | HO-LY GHOST ;
As it was in the beginning, is now, and | e-ver shall be : world without | end. A-men.

Choir *ANTIPHON*

Come, O LORD, and vis - it us in peace, that we may re -
- joice be - fore Thee with a per - fect heart. Al - le - lu - - ia.
ADD IN EASTER-TIDE

Choir
Priest
CHRIST, have mercy upon us.
LORD, have mercy upon us.
Priest
LORD, have mercy up - on us.

Priest and Choir *LORD'S PRAYER*

Our FA-THER, which art in Heaven, Hallowed be Thy Name. Thy kingdom come. Thy will be done in earth, As it is in Heaven. Give us this day our daily bread. And forgive us our trespasses, As we forgive them that trespass against us.

Choir
Priest
℟ But deliver us from e - vil. A - men.
℣ And lead us not into temp - ta - tion.

Priest and Choir *CREED*

I believe in GOD, the FATHER Almighty, Maker of Heaven and earth:

And in JESUS CHRIST His only SON our LORD, Who was conceived by the HOLY GHOST, Born of the Virgin Mary, Suffered under Pontius Pilate, Was crucified, dead, and buried, He descended into hell; The third day He rose again from the dead, He ascended into Heaven, And sitteth on the right hand of GOD the FATHER Almighty; From thence He shall come to judge the quick and the dead.

I believe in the HOLY GHOST; the Holy Catholick Church; The Communion of Saints; The Forgiveness of sins;

Choir
Priest
℟ And the life ever - last - ing. A - men.
℣ The resurrection of the bo - dy.

Priest
℣ Blessed art Thou, O Lord God of our Fa - thers.
Choir
℟ And to be praised and exalted above all for e - ver.
Priest
℣ Blessed is Thy glorious and ho - ly Name.
Choir
℟ And to be praised and exalted above all for e - ver.
Priest
℣ Blessed art Thou, O Lord, in the firmament of Hea - ven.
Choir
℟ And above all to be praised and glorified for e - ver.
Priest
℣ The Lord bless us and keep us.
Choir
℟ A - - - men.

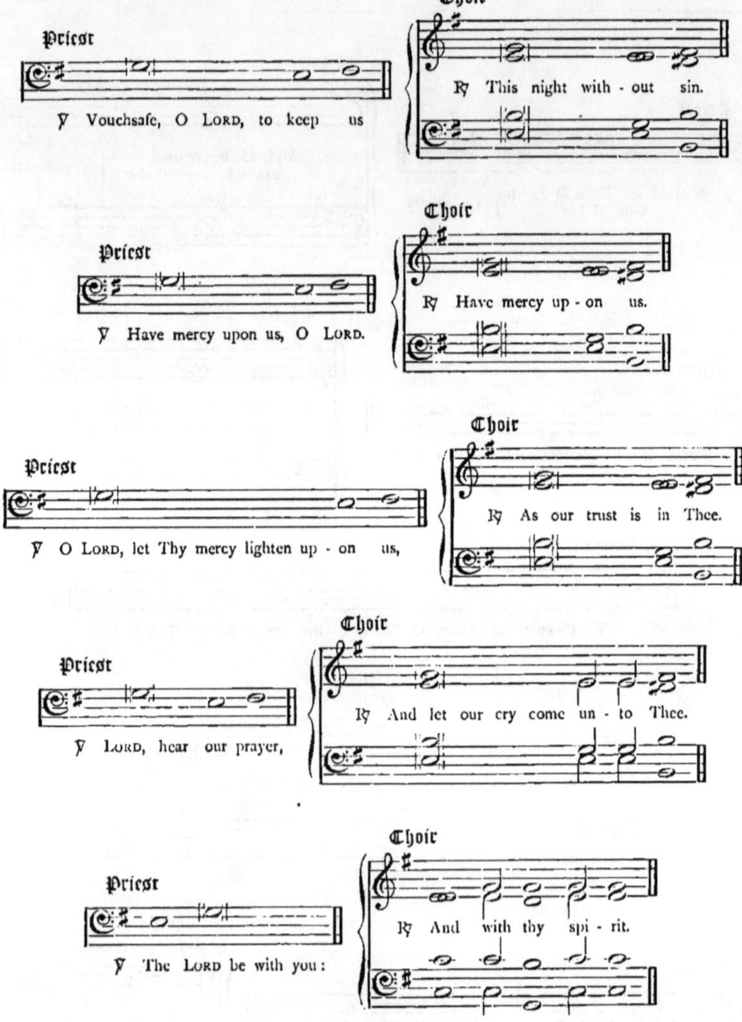
Priest
℣ Vouchsafe, O Lord, to keep us
Choir
℟ This night with - out sin.
Priest
℣ Have mercy upon us, O Lord.
Choir
℟ Have mercy up - on us.
Priest
℣ O Lord, let Thy mercy lighten up - on us,
Choir
℟ As our trust is in Thee.
Priest
℣ Lord, hear our prayer,
Choir
℟ And let our cry come un - to Thee.
Priest
℣ The Lord be with you:
Choir
℟ And with thy spi - rit.

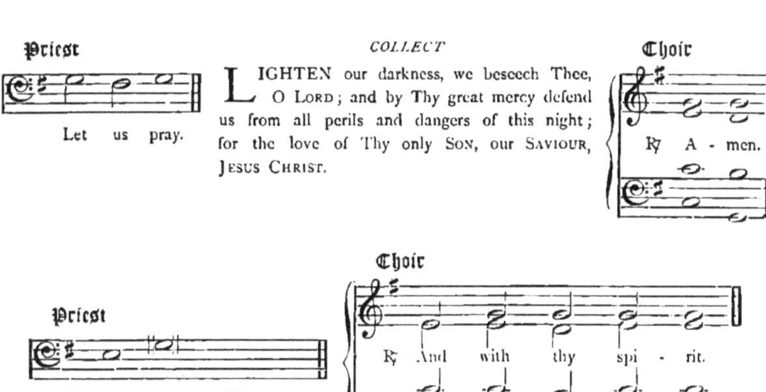
Priest
Let us pray.
Choir
℟ A - men.

COLLECT

LIGHTEN our darkness, we beseech Thee, O LORD; and by Thy great mercy defend us from all perils and dangers of this night; for the love of Thy only SON, our SAVIOUR, JESUS CHRIST.

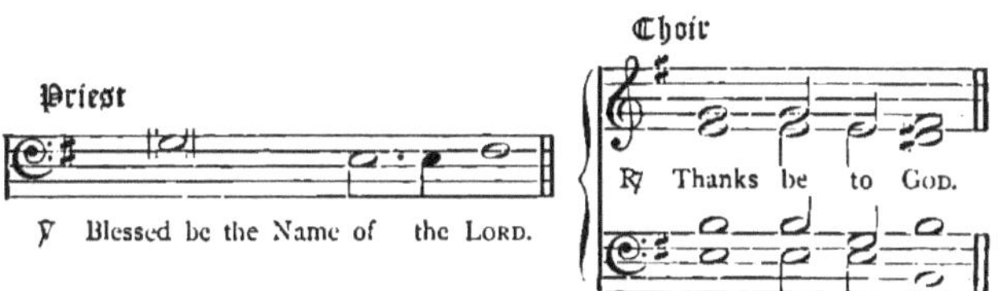
Priest
℣ The LORD be with you.
Choir
℟ And with thy spi - rit.

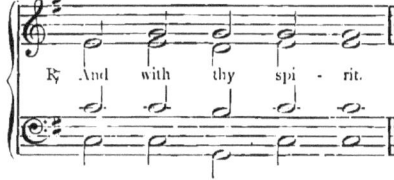

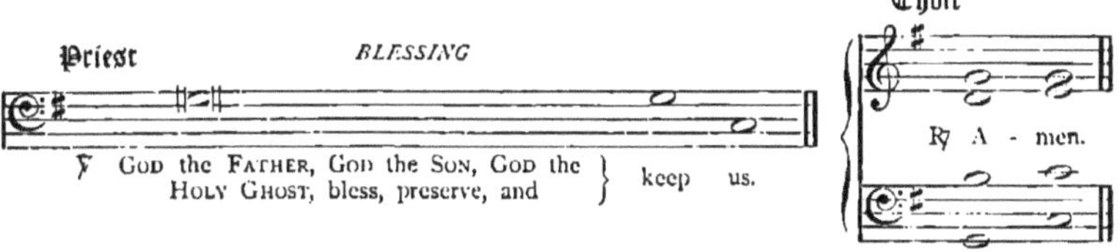
Priest
℣ Blessed be the Name of the LORD.
Choir
℟ Thanks be to GOD.

Priest *BLESSING*

℣ GOD the FATHER, GOD the SON, GOD the HOLY GHOST, bless, preserve, and keep us.

Choir

℟ A - men.

www.ingramcontent.com/pod-product-compliance
Lightning Source LLC
Chambersburg PA
CBHW030553270326
41927CB00007B/904

* 9 7 8 3 3 3 7 3 7 2 4 8 4 *